24.6.17.
Fr. 1.–

Lovestories 4 Girls

First Love on a Rainy Day

Julia Ross

Compact Verlag

Bisher sind in dieser Reihe erschienen:

Band 1: Full Moon Kisses
Band 2: Last Chance for a First Date
Band 3: Flirt But Don't Fall in Love
Band 4: Trouble in Seventh Heaven
Band 5: Heartbreak Summer
Band 6: First Love on a Rainy Day

Weitere Titel sind in Vorbereitung.

Chefredaktion: Dr. Angela Sendlinger
Redaktion: Helga Aichele
Fachredaktion: Monika Bowler
Produktion: Wolfram Friedrich
Illustrationen: Bettina Weisl (MA Illustration)
Typografischer Entwurf: textum GmbH
Umschlaggestaltung: Bettina Weisl (MA Illustration)

ISBN: 978-3-8174-7845-3
7278451

Besuche uns im Internet: www.compactverlag.de

Vorwort

Mit dieser spannenden und romantischen Compact Lovestory kannst du deine Englischkenntnisse spielend leicht verbessern. Eine deutsche Einleitung vor jedem neuen Kapitel hilft dir, den englischen Text zu verstehen. Außerdem werden auf jeder Seite die etwas schwierigeren Wörter erklärt, und durch die Zeichnungen bekommst du eine genauere Vorstellung von den vier Girls und ihren aufregenden Erlebnissen. Blätter doch einfach mal durch!

Jedes Kapitel wird durch Übungen und Tests ergänzt, die richtig spannend und abwechslungsreich sind: Da geht es um Jungs und Liebe, Partys, Freundschaft und Mode – so wird Englisch lernen richtig spannend und cool!

Die Antworten und Lösungen kannst du gleich ins Buch schreiben und hinterher im Lösungsteil nachlesen, ob du alles richtig gemacht hast und was die Tests über dich aussagen. Und wenn du möchtest, kannst du alle Vokabeln im Glossar noch einmal nachschlagen. Slang-Ausdrücke sind mit einem ϟ gekennzeichnet.

Wir wünschen dir viel Spaß mit Evie und ihren Freundinnen – und natürlich viel Erfolg beim Englisch lernen!

Inhalt

1

Rain, Rain, Go Away

1

Eigentlich hatte sich Evie auf eine tolle Urlaubswoche am Meer gefreut, mit viel Sonne und noch mehr sportlichen Herausforderungen. Aber seit Tagen regnet es, und sie muss die ganze Zeit mit ihrer Familie im Wohnwagen verbringen. Allmählich fällt ihr die Decke auf den Kopf. Als dann bei einem Spaziergang im Regen auch noch der kleine Hund ihrer Großeltern verschwindet, ist Evie nur noch zum Heulen zumute. Doch Rettung naht ...

Evie looked out of the window at a landscape of blurred greens and greys. She looked across the fields, past the river and down to the beach and tried to work out where the sea began. In the heavy rain, the grey sky and the grey sea looked exactly the same and the raindrops that rolled down the glass made everything unclear.

"Rain, rain, go away, come again another day," sang Olly, her brother, in a silly voice. The words were from a nursery rhyme which Evie knew well.

"If the rain does go away, then I really hope it *doesn't* come again any time soon," muttered Evie. "We've been on holiday for nearly four days now and it still hasn't stopped raining yet. What a summer!"

"Ah yes, the wonderful English summer," added Olly sarcastically.

Evie's whole family, including her grandparents, were spending a week at a caravan site near the coast for their summer holiday. However, the endless rain that trickled down the caravan windows was ruining all of Evie's hopes for a fun week away in the August sunshine.

blurred	verschwommen, undeutlich
nursery rhyme	Kinderlied
to mutter	murmeln
caravan site	Wohnwagenpark
to trickle	tröpfeln, rinnen
ϟ washout	Reinfall
stuck	festsitzend
to stare at	anstarren
ϟ How on earth...?	Wie in aller Welt ...?
ridiculous	lächerlich
grumpy	brummig, mürrisch

Instead, the holiday was turning into a complete washout. Stuck in their caravan all day, Evie and her brothers were beginning to argue much more than usual. On top of that, Evie was extremely bored. Normally, she was quite an active person, playing sports outdoors and seeing her friends. But with so much rain, how could she play sports? The only activity anyone could suggest was yet another game of cards.

"I know," Evie said, almost shouting. She was still staring at the wet scene in front of her. "Let's have a race!"

"How on earth are we going to have a race in here?" asked her oldest brother Max. "Don't be so ridiculous."

"Don't be so grumpy!" replied Evie angrily.

It seemed as if Max had been in a bad mood ever since he got back from his gap year in Australia. He was always talking about the fantastic weather and the beautiful beaches he had seen there. He seemed in an even worse mood now that he was experiencing the exact opposite at home in England.

"I didn't mean a real race anyway," Evie continued. "I meant a raindrop race. Everyone has to pick one of these raindrops here on the window and if yours gets to the bottom first, you win."

Her brothers agreed to play the game, and soon they were all cheering for their raindrops as they trickled down the glass.

gap year	freies Jahr nach dem Schulabschluss
to cheer	anfeuern, jubeln
to cheat	mogeln, betrügen
to admit	zugeben
to insist	beharren, bestehen auf

"Yes! I won!" shouted Simon, who was the second oldest of the four.

"No, you didn't!" Max argued. "That was a different raindrop to the one you picked. You cheated!"

"I did not! You just don't want to admit that you came last!" Simon replied.

"That doesn't matter anyway because mine clearly got to the bottom first," insisted Olly.

The argument continued until all four of them were shouting at each other at the same time. Even their grandparents' puppy, Tilly, joined in and yapped loudly.

puppy	Welpe
to join in	mitmachen
to yap	kläffen
⚡ How about ...?	Wie wär's mit ...?
to sigh	seufzen
to beep	piepen

Soon, their father cried out above the noise of the argument:
"Enough! Calm down, all of you! I know that everyone is disappointed with this bad weather, but we can still have fun indoors without shouting at each other like small children."
"How about we try out the entertainment this evening?" suggested Evie's mother, trying to be helpful. "There's a magic show on at six o'clock here at the hall. We could all go together."
Everyone agreed that the show sounded better than another evening of card games and television. It was already nearly half past five, so there would not be long to wait. Even so, time seemed to pass so slowly that Evie sighed when she looked at the clock and went back to watch the rain.
Suddenly, her mobile phone beeped. She picked it up quickly, excited to read the message.

> Hello from sunny Florida! I'm having such a good time here – we went to Disneyland today! Our hotel has a huge pool and an amazing restaurant. Aren't summer holidays brilliant?! Lots of love, Emily x

Evie wanted to feel happy for her best friend Emily, but instead, she fought hard to stop herself from feeling angry. Why did Emily's family go on such exciting holidays, when she had to shelter from the rain in a dingy caravan? It did not seem fair.

She sighed again and put down her phone. She knew that it was not Emily's fault that her holiday had everything that Evie's did not. She looked at the clock again. Only a minute had passed.

to shelter from	Schutz suchen vor
dingy	schäbig, düster

ÜBUNG 1: Match-up. Verbinde die Wörter, die inhaltlich zusammenpassen!

1. skiing	beach
2. sunbathing	race
3. camping	sunshine
4. bad weather	snow
5. swimming	tent
6. summer	rain
7. raindrop	sea

Eventually, it was time for the magic show. The whole family ran to the entertainment hall as the rain poured down on them. By the time they got there, Evie's umbrella had been blown inside out by the wind and her short hair was a mess of wet spikes.

They dried themselves as best they could and took their seats to watch the show.

eventually	schließlich, letztendlich
to pour down	herabströmen
inside out	verkehrt herum
mess	Durcheinander
spike	*hier:* Stachel
ragged	zerfetzt, zerlumpt
cape	Umhang
volunteer	Freiwilliger

A short man with long, dirty blond hair came onto the stage. He was wearing a rather ragged cape and a tall hat that looked very old.

"Ladies and gentlemen, boys and girls, welcome to an evening of magic and mystery," he said in a strange voice that did not sound like his own.

"I am Marvelon the Magician, and I have many powers, as you will see. I have the power to see the inside of your mind. In a moment I will show you this. But first, I need a volunteer. How about you, young man?"

Evie realized with horror that he was pointing at her. She knew that her hair looked a mess after the rain, but she was sure that she still looked like a girl.

"Um... I'm actually a girl," she said shyly. "But okay, I'll volunteer."
Marvelon looked a little embarrassed, but got out a pack of cards, ready for his first trick.
"Pick a card, any card, young lady," he said to Evie.
She took one of the cards and showed it to the audience. It was the queen of diamonds.
Marvelon looked as if he was thinking hard. He closed his eyes, put his hands together and finally said, "Your card is... the queen of diamonds!"
The audience clapped softly.

embarrassed	verlegen
audience	Publikum
queen of diamonds	Karodame (Kartenspiel)
to clap	(Beifall) klatschen
accidentally	versehentlich
face up	mit dem Motiv nach oben
to scramble	hasten, stürzen
to roll one's eyes	die Augen verdrehen

Evie turned to go back to her seat, but accidentally stepped on Marvelon's foot. He dropped his cards as he moved back out of her way. They fell to the ground, face up. Every single one of them was the queen of diamonds.
"Uh... on to the next trick," Marvelon said quickly while he scrambled to pick up the cards. "I will make a rabbit appear from a hat!"
He placed a hat on the table and began to talk about his magical powers. However, as he talked, the hat started to

move. It moved further and further, until, just when Marvelon turned around to begin the trick, the hat fell off the table. A white rabbit jumped out of it and ran into the audience.

Evie rolled her eyes. "Thanks for suggesting something to do," she told her mum and dad, "but I think I'm going to go and read for a bit. I'll be in the caravan."

Her parents' reply was cut short, because at that moment the rabbit suddenly ran underneath her mum's chair. Evie began to ask her brothers if they wanted to go back with her, but stopped herself when she noticed the three of them almost fall off their seats with laughter. At least somebody is enjoying the show, she thought.

ÜBUNG 2: Multiple choice. Kreuze jeweils die richtige Variante an!

1. Evie's umbrella was blown...
   a) ❑ inside-out
   b) ❑ upside-down
   by the wind.

2. The magician's clothes looked...
   a) ❑ old and worn out.
   b) ❑ filthy.

3. For his trick, Marvelon needed...
   a) ❑ an assistant.
   b) ❑ a volunteer.

4. Marvelon mistook Evie...
   a) ❑ as
   b) ❑ for
   a boy.

5. When Marvelon dropped the cards, they landed...
   a) ❑ face up.
   b) ❑ top up.

6. The rabbit...
   a) ❑ rescued
   b) ❑ escaped
   from the hat.

When Evie got back to the caravan, she picked up her book and tried to read, but she could not concentrate. She was feeling extremely restless without her usual football practice or her friends around.

It was not raining so heavily any more, so she decided to go for a walk until the rest of her family returned. But when she stepped outside, her grandparents' puppy ran out of the caravan behind her, wagging her tail.

"No, Tilly! Get back inside!"

But the dog just stared at Evie with her big, dark eyes. She seemed to want to come with her.

Evie looked at Tilly. Spending so much time in that dingy caravan was probably just as hard for Tilly as it was for her, Evie thought. But she also knew how protective her grandparents were of their new puppy. They would never let her take Tilly for a walk on her own.

"You can't come with me, Tilly," she said.

The puppy still looked up at her hopefully, still wagging her tail.

Evie could not help but feel sorry for the dog. She decided to take her out after all, just for one short

restless	unruhig
to wag one's tail	mit dem Schwanz wedeln
protective	beschützerisch, fürsorglich
after all	*hier:* dennoch

walk. That way her grandparents would never find out, and Tilly would not have to be stuck indoors all day. If Tilly was on a dog lead, she could not possibly get into trouble.
Evie began to walk along the river that cut through the caravan site and then gradually widened to join the stormy sea. She felt as if she was the only person around, even though in the distance she could see a few dark figures with surfboards. Although the sky was still grey, her mood was getting better. She took her mobile phone out of her pocket and called her friend Holly.
"Evie!" answered Holly. "How's your holiday going? I hope it hasn't been raining as much as it has here at home!"
"Well," Evie replied, "it looks as if it's about to stop raining right now at least, so maybe tomorrow won't be so bad."
"What a shame about the weather," said Holly sympathetically. "I hope it gets better soon. Anyway, have you met any nice boys yet?"
"No! The only person I've met here so far was a weird old magician who thought *I* was a boy!"

dog lead	Hundeleine
gradually	allmählich
to widen	breiter werden
figure	Gestalt
sympathetically	mitfühlend
weird	merkwürdig
to break up with sb.	mit jmd. Schluss machen
to realize	erkennen, begreifen
to work out	funktionieren
collar	*hier:* Halsband
nowhere to be seen	nirgends zu sehen

"Oh dear!" said Holly. "Still, you only broke up with Nick a little while ago, so maybe it's too early for romance."
"Yeah, maybe," agreed Evie, looking into the distance.
She still kind of missed Nick, she realized. They had dated for quite some time and had had a great time together because they both loved the same things. But somehow their relationship hadn't worked out.
"I do miss having a boyfriend a bit," Evie told Holly, "especially now that I'm stuck here with nothing to do."
"Better to have no boyfriend than to have the wrong boyfriend. Anyway, I'm sure you'll meet someone nice soon."
Evie laughed. "Definitely not around here! Anyway, how are things back at home?"
"Good, thanks," Holly replied. "I've just been spending most of my time with Dan. Pretty boring, really!"
Even without seeing her face, Evie could tell that Holly was smiling. Evie liked Daniel and knew that he made her friend very happy.
"Sounds lovely. Anyway, I should probably go," she added. She remembered that she had planned to take Tilly back quickly.
After she had said goodbye and put her phone back in her pocket, Evie turned around to walk back to the caravan. The dog lead felt lighter than before. She looked down and felt her heart drop into her stomach: at the end of the lead there was just an empty collar! Tilly was nowhere to be seen.

ÜBUNG 3: What is your perfect pet? Finde heraus, welches Haustier am besten zu dir passt!

1. Would you be likely to lose your pet as Evie did?
   a) ❑ Yes. I couldn't even look after a plant.
   b) ❑ No, I wouldn't. If I had a pet, I would look after it very carefully.
   c) ❑ No. I would keep my pet in a safe place, so it could not escape.

2. How much time and effort would you spend on your pet?
   a) ❑ Not very much, I'm too busy.
   b) ❑ A lot. I would give it a lot of attention.
   c) ❑ I would spend the time and money that it needed. I would find out all about how to look after it properly.

3. Would you mind if you had to feed your pet something disgusting?
   a) ❑ I wouldn't want to feed my pet unless the food was clean and dry.
   b) ❑ Not unless it was really disgusting.
   c) ❑ No. I would feed it anything.

Evie picked up the collar, which now looked too large for such a small puppy. She realized too late that Tilly must have been small enough to get out of the collar while she had been talking to Holly.

"Oh no," Evie said out loud. Her heart was pounding.

Tilly was too young and helpless to be outdoors all alone and Evie knew that her grandparents would be incredibly upset if anything happened to their puppy.

She frantically looked across the fields. Surely, the little dog could not have gone far. Evie started to run back towards the caravan site. With every step, she became more and more worried, because Tilly was still nowhere to be seen.

Ten minutes later, Evie was in despair. She had run all the way to the family's caravan and back but still had not seen or heard the dog. By now, she was feeling extremely worried. After calling out Tilly's name once again, she did not know what else to do, so she sat down in the wet grass and began to cry.

A minute later, she felt a hand on her shoulder.

"Are you alright?" asked a gentle voice behind her.

to pound	pochen, klopfen
incredibly	unglaublich
frantically	hektisch, angestrengt
to be in despair	verzweifelt sein

When Evie looked up, she saw that the voice belonged to a boy with blond hair, who was wearing a black wetsuit and was carrying a surfboard.
"Is there anything I can do to help?"
Evie hated it when anybody saw her cry. She hoped that the light rain that was still falling would help to disguise her tears.

wetsuit	Neoprenanzug
to disguise sth.	etw. verbergen
comforting	tröstlich, beruhigend
to whistle	pfeifen
to spot	erblicken, entdecken
trapped	gefangen
to be swept away	fortgespült werden
current	Strömung

"It's alright, I don't need help," she said, as she tried to hide her emotions. "I've just lost my dog. ...Except that it isn't really mine, it's my grandparents'... and... and it's only a little puppy." As hard as she tried, she could not stop another tear from rolling down her face and falling onto the grass in front of her while she explained what had happened.
"Try not to worry," the boy told her. "Your grandparents' dog must be around here somewhere. I can help you find it if you want?"
Evie had not wanted him to help her, but his kind expression and soft voice were so comforting that she soon agreed that they should look for Tilly together.
"Have you tried whistling to her?" he asked.

Evie shook her head without saying anything.
He began to whistle and moments later, Evie heard a familiar yapping. They both ran towards where the sound had come from. Together, they ran along the river, until they finally spotted Tilly. The tiny puppy was trapped on a small rock in the middle of the water. It looked as though she might be swept away by the strong current at any moment.

ÜBUNG 4: Find the word. Welche Vokabel ist gemeint?

1. to beat quickly and loudly ....
2. to hide something ....
3. a feeling of hopelessness ....
4. wear this when you go surfing ....
5. a band put around a dog's neck ....
6. to end a relationship ....
7. to get wider ....
8. in a very hectic way ....
9. wanting to protect ....

Evie put her hand to her mouth in shock. "She must have tried to swim, but she's still too young and not very strong. We have to save her!"
The boy immediately got into the water, fighting the current. He reached the rock, picked Tilly up and held her close to his chest before swimming back to where Evie stood. Gently, the boy put Tilly in her arms. The tiny dog was completely wet and shivering, but she was still wagging her tail.
"Thank you so much!" Evie said to the boy. "I don't want to think about what could have happened if you hadn't come over to help me."
"No problem," he replied. "By the way, my name is Connor. I'm staying at that caravan site just up there with my family."
"Me too! And my name's Evie. I'm very pleased to meet you!"
Connor laughed. "You too! Why don't we go back to the caravan site – it looks as if that little dog would be quite happy to go back inside again."

They walked back together, talking about their holidays. Connor told her that in spite of the rain, he did not like to stay indoors, so he had been surfing at the beach every day. Soon they reached Evie's caravan.

When she looked at Connor properly for the first time, Evie realized how attractive he was. She had been so worried and emotional before that she had not even noticed what he looked like. Now, as she looked up, she saw a handsome face with a strong jaw, framed by messy, curly blond hair.

chest	Brust
to shiver	zittern
properly	richtig, genau
jaw	Kiefer
framed by	umrahmt von
messy	durcheinander, unordentlich
curly	lockig
knight in shining armour	Retter in der Not

"I guess I'll see you around here then," she said. "Or maybe down at the beach surfing."

"Yeah, why don't you come along next time and surf with me?" Connor suggested. "I can check if you're around before I go tomorrow."

"Sounds cool," replied Evie. She would never say no to the chance to try out a new sport. "And thanks again for saving Tilly. You're her knight in shining armour!"

After saying goodbye, Evie took Tilly back into the caravan. Luckily, her family had not yet returned, but they would be back soon. Tilly was very wet and Evie knew that she must act immediately or her grandparents would guess that something had happened to her. She tried to dry Tilly with a towel, but even then Tilly still looked suspiciously damp.

suspiciously	verdächtig
damp	feucht
screen	*hier:* Trennwand
to be supposed to do sth.	eigentlich etw. tun sollen
out of tune	*hier:* schief, falsch
ϟ sis (sister)	Schwesterherz
to quicken	schneller werden
to wipe	wischen
neighbouring	benachbart

Evie looked at her hair-dryer, which was lying on the bed. She wondered if she could use it to dry Tilly. Eventually, she decided that Tilly had had enough adventures for one day.

A little later, while Evie was reading her book, her family returned to the caravan. They were all talking together loudly.

"That was so bad that it was almost good," Olly said to Simon, as he walked through the door.

"I think my favourite trick was when he tried to make that lady disappear, and the screen that she was supposed to hide behind fell down."

"No, the funniest bit was definitely the song at the end," said Simon, laughing at the memory. "Could it be maaaa-gic?" he sang in a funny, out-of-tune voice.

"Sis, you really missed a great show," Olly said to Evie. "Much better than reading in here, anyway. You must have been so bored."

Evie did not say anything.
"Oh Tilly, you're all damp!" shouted her grandmother suddenly. Evie felt her heartbeat quicken.
"You silly little dog!" Evie's grandmother continued. "You've jumped in your water bowl again!"
"She's always doing that," said Evie's grandfather. "I think she likes water."
Again, Evie stayed silent. Tilly probably won't like water so much any more, she thought.

The next day, Connor stopped at Evie's caravan on his way to the beach.
"Look," he said when she opened the door. "The sun's come out for you today. Perfect weather for surfing, don't you think?"
They only had Connor's surfboard, but he let her use it for most of the morning while he showed her what to do. Evie had so much fun that she forgot about how cold the sea was and did not feel embarrassed at all about falling off the board a few times. Instead, she laughed with him, shook her wet hair and wiped the salty water from her eyes.
They spent most of the day together and soon realized that they had many things in common. They even lived in neighbouring towns, which made Evie feel hopeful that they would see each other again after their holiday had ended. When they walked home from the beach at the end of the afternoon, Connor offered Evie his jumper to keep

her warm. As she put it on, she noticed how good it smelt. Back in the caravan, Evie's parents were surprised by the change they noticed in her. Rather than complain about how boring their summer holiday was and argue with her brothers, Evie now seemed to be constantly smiling. She was happy to play cards with her grandparents that evening and even helped with the household chores without being asked. Evie's family guessed that the change in the weather must have cheered her up. However, they were still surprised when Evie said that she wished they could stay a bit longer.

ÜBUNG 5: Unscramble the words. Ordne die Buchstaben in Klammern zu sinnvollen Wörtern!

1. Evie and her family were staying in a *(narvaca)* ....
2. Connor and Evie shared a *(sorfbadur)* .... on the beach.
3. The *(wearthe)* .... was getting better.
4. Tilly belonged to Evie's *(dartspengarn)* ....
5. Connor *(veads)* .... Tilly when she was in *(nardeg)* ....

Evie now looked forward to each new day at the caravan site because she knew that it would be full of fun and laughter with Connor. She was beginning to feel something that she had never felt before every time she looked at his handsome face or heard his soft voice.

Before long, the final day of her holiday arrived. The family planned to leave in the morning, but Connor had not yet come to meet Evie. Her parents kept telling her to hurry up and to put her things in the car. However, Evie could only think about saying goodbye to Connor. Eventually, she threw the last of her things into the car and ran off to his caravan to find him.

"Evie!" shouted her father. "Come back, we have to leave in five minutes!"

She barely heard him as she ran. She knocked on the door of the caravan, and Connor came out, half dressed and looking sleepy. As she looked at him, Evie felt quite weak.

rather than	anstatt
constantly	ständig
household chores	Hausarbeit
to cheer sb. up	jmd. aufmuntern
barely	kaum

"I'm about to go home," she explained. "But I couldn't leave without saying goodbye."

Connor looked disappointed. "I thought I would get to see you again today. But before you go, there's something that I need to do as well."

It was raining heavily again, and Evie stood shivering beneath the grey storm clouds. Connor held her tight and kissed her while the rain poured down on them. Evie felt the warmth of his kiss and of his skin next to hers. She felt as if she was exploding inside with happiness.

to hold sb. tight	jmd. fest umarmen

As she turned to leave, she paused. "Wait!" she suddenly shouted. "I don't even have your phone number! I can't believe I didn't think of it sooner."

"You're right. I really want to see you again, Evie. Call me later and we'll arrange something."

ÜBUNG 6: Choose the right word! Unterstreiche jeweils die richtige Variante.

1. Evie was starting to feel something/nothing/anything that she had never felt before.
2. The final day of the holiday arrived sooner than Evie have/has/had expected.
3. Evies/Evie's/Evies' parents told her to hurry up and get ready to leave.
4. Evie could not leave the caravan site except/without/between saying goodbye to Connor.
5. Connor wrote/writed/wroted his phone number on a piece of paper.

Connor quickly wrote his phone number on a piece of paper and handed it to Evie.
"See you again soon," she shouted, as she ran back to the car. She was so happy that she was barely aware of the rain that soaked her.

"Evie, what were you thinking?" shouted her father. "Get in the car, we're leaving right now."
She watched the blurry scene from out of the car window. As they drove away from the caravan site, she thought that she could make out a blond boy waving at her through the rain.

to be aware of sth.	etw. bemerken
to soak	durchweichen
blurry	verschwommen
to make out	ausmachen, erspähen
to wave	winken

2

The Calm Before the Storm

2

Evie ist total in Connor verliebt und überglücklich. Sie kann es kaum erwarten, ihn wiederzusehen. Zu Hause angekommen, trifft sie sich sofort mit ihren Freundinnen, um ihnen alles über ihren Schwarm zu erzählen.
Doch als sie Connor anrufen will und den Zettel mit seiner Telefonnummer aus der Tasche zieht, ist die Nummer vom Regen völlig unleserlich geworden! Nicht einmal der klugen Emily gelingt es, die Nummer zu entziffern. Evie ist verzweifelt: Wie soll sie Connor jetzt wiedersehen?

Evie smiled all the way through the journey home. Her brothers had guessed that her unusually good mood had something to do with her new friendship with Connor. But even when they made fun of her, Evie could not hide her happiness. Instead, she just looked out of the window and daydreamed about her first telephone conversation with Connor. Then suddenly she remembered something – she still had not replied to Emily's text message. Quickly, Evie typed her reply:

hi ems! glad ur having such a gr8 time. summer hols r brilliant, i agree! met a gorgeous boy @ the caravan site, think it could b the start of something special... love, EV x

When the car pulled up outside her house, Evie could not help but feel disappointed to be home again after such a romantic week away. However, she looked forward to seeing her friends again and wanted to tell them everything that had happened. She knew that Emily would be returning from her holiday in America within a few days. Even better, her two other best friends, Holly and Nina, were at home already: she could invite them to come over for a chat. Besides, Connor did not live far away, so she would soon be able to experience the wonderful feelings of the last week all over again.

text message	SMS
ϟ hols (holidays)	Ferien
gorgeous	umwerfend, großartig
to pull up	*hier:* anhalten
chat	Plauderei
besides	außerdem

As soon as she got inside the house, Evie called Nina and Holly and told them about her holiday romance. She also asked them if they would like to come over. They could not wait to ask her more questions and quickly agreed to come over to her house within half an hour.

ÜBUNG 7: Unscramble the phone call. Bringe das Telefongespräch in die richtige Reihenfolge!

a) "I think so, too! Anyway, do you want to come over to my house in half an hour?"

b) "Brilliant, thank you, Nina! I met a really amazing guy..."

c) "He sounds perfect for you!"

d) "Of course! I want to hear all about Connor."

e) "Wow! What's his name?"

f) "Okay, see you later then. Bye!"

g) "Hi Evie, how was your holiday?"

h) "He's called Connor. He's really into surfing and other sports. We had so much fun together!"

1	2	3	4	5	6	7	8
g							

"So, tell us EVERYTHING!" said Holly, as her brown eyes lit up with excitement.
She was the most romantic of the four girls and there was no detail, no matter how small, that she did not want to know about when one of her friends had a crush on somebody.

"Yeah, tell us all about this amazing guy!" added Nina. "I've never heard you sound so head over heels in love before!"

to light up	aufleuchten, strahlen
no matter how	egal wie
ϟ to have a crush on sb.	in jmd. verknallt sein
head over heels in love	Hals über Kopf verliebt
dimple	Grübchen
cheek	Wange
to giggle	kichern

"I know," Evie said. Her face was a picture of happiness. "I just feel... different when I'm with him. It seems right somehow."
"So, what's he like?" Holly asked.
"Connor's funny, and kind, and very good-looking! He's a little older than me and really tall; he has quite long blond hair. And when he smiles, he has a dimple on his left cheek. Oh... and he's a really good kisser!"
They all giggled.
"So, when are you going to see him again?" asked Holly.
"I don't know exactly," Evie said. "But soon, I think. He asked me to call him tonight to arrange something. In fact, that reminds me – I should put that phone number in a safe place."

She reached down and pulled out the folded piece of paper from the pocket of her dark jeans. The other two girls looked at each other with worried expressions when they saw how crumpled and damp the paper was.

"Here it is!" Evie said happily. She unfolded the sheet of paper and held it up to look at the phone number written down.

The three girls all gasped at the same time. Evie stared at the paper in horror. The rain had soaked through it and had blurred all of the ink. All that was left of the number was a large blue shape in the middle of the piece of paper.

The sickening feeling in the bottom of Evie's stomach was even worse than it had been when she had lost Tilly by the river.

"Wait," Holly said quickly. "It's okay, I'm sure he'll call you if he doesn't hear from you soon. You can't both have lost each other's numbers!"

Evie shook her head sadly. "He doesn't have my number. Everything happened so quickly... I know this sounds ridiculous, but... but I don't even know his surname."

"What?! But you liked each other so much!" exclaimed Holly. She simply could not believe that Evie had not been more sensible.

"I know that, Holly!" Evie snapped. "It's just that I wasn't thinking clearly at the time. I was so busy having such a good time that, well, I didn't think about anything else."

Nina tried to calm down the situation. "Let's try not to worry right now. There must be a way around this problem."

"She's right," Holly agreed. "How about searching for him online?"

It seemed like a good idea, so Evie tried to remember all of the details that she knew about Connor and then used them to look for him on the Internet. But every search brought back thousands of results.

"Okay, this isn't going to work," Holly finally admitted.

Nina agreed. "But there must be other things you can do. Anyway, I'm sure Emily will be able to help when she gets back from her holiday. She's so clever, she's sure to work out what to do."

folded	gefaltet
crumpled	zerknittert
to gasp	nach Luft ringen
shape	Gebilde, Form
sickening	scheußlich, ekelhaft
to exclaim	ausrufen
sensible	vernünftig
to snap	jmd. anschnauzen

ÜBUNG 8: Who said what? Ordne die Sätze dem richtigen Mädchen zu!

1. ❑ Nina asked...
2. ❑ Evie explained that...
3. ❑ Holly asked,...
4. ❑ Evie snapped,...
5. ❑ Holly said,...

a) "You can't both have lost each other's numbers!"
b) "So, when are you going to see him next?"
c) she had never felt the same way about a boy before.
d) Evie to tell her all about the amazing guy she had met.
e) "I know that, Holly!"

Evie always looked forward to seeing her best friend Emily when they had spent even a few days apart, but this time the waiting was even harder than usual.
The following days passed slowly. Evie tried to lose herself in her favourite sports, but she did not seem to find her usual energy. One day she was playing with her football in the garden, when she kicked the ball half-heartedly and sat down on the grass with her head in her hands. Her brother Olly saw her and went over to ask her what was wrong.
"It's Connor," she said sadly.

apart	getrennt
to lose oneself in	sich ablenken mit
half-heartedly	halbherzig
miserable	unglücklich
comment	Bemerkung
tan	Sonnenbräune

"Hasn't he called?" Olly asked.

"Well, no," she replied. "That's the problem – Connor doesn't have my number and I've lost his. So no, he hasn't called."

Saying the words out loud only seemed to make Evie more upset. For reasons that even she did not understand, she was also beginning to feel very angry and annoyed with Olly. Couldn't he see that she did not want to talk about this?

"What about finding him on the Internet?" Olly asked.

"Oh, go away," Evie snapped. "You don't understand."

Olly looked hurt but left her alone. Evie felt so miserable that she just sat in the grass and tried hard not to cry.

Three days later, Emily was walking over to Evie's house, wearing a new outfit that she had bought in Florida. She had had a wonderful holiday and could not wait to tell Evie all about it. But as soon as the front door opened, Evie took Emily inside without even saying "hello" and showed her a crumpled piece of paper. Evie was talking very fast and barely managed to make a quick comment about Emily's tan before she started to explain her problem.

Emily looked at the paper for a few seconds while Evie waited impatiently.
Eventually, Emily said in a serious tone of voice, "I think this could be just like cracking a code. If you look very hard, you can still make out the shapes of the numbers. I'll just need to analyze the paper carefully..."
Evie felt more hopeful than she had done in days. Maybe her friends were right, and Emily *was* clever enough to find a solution to her unusual problem. She sat down close to Emily and took out a pen and paper, ready to write down any numbers that Emily might manage to find in the blurry blue shape on the page.
"Well, all mobile numbers start with 07, so we know the first two numbers already," Emily said confidently. "I can use that knowledge to help me understand how the blurring has changed the shape of the numbers. Look! I can already find two more zeros in there!"
Evie could not believe it: Emily was cracking the code.
"And there's a 3. It has to be," Emily continued. "And the next number is... uh... 9?"

to crack a code	einen Code knacken
to analyze	analysieren, untersuchen
confidently	zuversichtlich
uncertainty	Unsicherheit
It's no good.	Es bringt nichts.
hug	Umarmung
to mirror	widerspiegeln
fate	Schicksal

Evie did not like the note of uncertainty in Emily's voice.
"Right, the next one... um... Q?"

"Q?!" cried Evie. "This is supposed to be a phone number, Emily – it has to be a *number*!"
"Oh, right. Sorry," Emily said. She looked at the page for a little while longer before she added, "It's no good, Evie, I'm really sorry. I could probably tell you half of the numbers, but without the other half it's useless."
The hope that Evie had felt earlier all disappeared. The disappointment that now replaced it was much worse than the frustration that she had felt before. Emily noticed her friend's sad expression and moved closer to give her a comforting hug.
"Oh Emily, how will I ever be able to see him again?"
"I don't know," Emily replied. Her face mirrored Evie's sadness. "...But if he is the boy you are meant to be with, then fate will bring you back together again."
For someone so clever, Emily really has some rather silly ideas, Evie thought to herself miserably. How can this be fate? There's no such thing as fate.

ÜBUNG 9: True or false? Kreuze die richtigen Aussagen an!

1. Evie played sports to try to forget about her problem. ❑
2. Emily went to Evie's house to talk about her holiday in Florida. ❑
3. Evie was looking forward to hearing about Emily's holiday. ❑
4. Emily did not really try to help Evie. ❑
5. Emily managed to find out Connor's number. ❑
6. Evie did not believe that fate would bring her and Connor back together. ❑
7. Evie believes in fate. ❑

Still half asleep, Evie rubbed her eyes and tried to pay attention. She had become used to late nights and lie-ins during the summer holidays, so getting up this morning had been really difficult.

It was the first day back at school. Evie's teacher, Mrs Skelton, was talking in a loud voice, but Evie wasn't listening – at least, not until Mrs Skelton mentioned a test. When she heard the word "test", Evie groaned, as did the rest of the class.

⚡ lie-in	Ausschlafen
to groan	stöhnen
effort	Anstrengung
to revise	wiederholen, lernen
to complete	ausfüllen, beenden

"Calm down everyone, it's not *that* kind of test!" the teacher continued. "It's not a test of knowledge – it is a test of your interests, which will help you to find your ideal job. You can use computers, so even on the first day back at school, this shouldn't be too much of an effort for you. Okay, get ready everyone, the test should take about ten minutes."

Evie did not feel much like doing any sort of test, but once she had started to answer the questions, she found that they were quite interesting. She had never thought about her ideal job before, but now she began to wonder what the results of the test would suggest for her.

Emily must really want to know, too, because she was choosing her answers very quickly. She seemed a little stressed, as though this was a real test and she had forgotten to revise. Meanwhile, Holly was completing the test very slowly, because she had to think hard about every question and ask her friends for their opinions. She could be very indecisive sometimes.

Emily finished the test first, and the other three girls moved nearer to Emily's computer to look at the results.

"Back to your own tests, girls," said Mrs Skelton.

They returned to their seats, but could not stay quiet for long.

"It told me that I should be a scientist!" said Emily happily, trying not to speak too loudly.

indecisive	unentschlossen
scientist	Wissenschaftlerin
translator	Übersetzerin
shriek of excitement	aufgeregter Schrei
to attract a glare	einen wütenden Blick ernten
deep in thought	ganz in Gedanken

Nina was next to finish. "It says my ideal job would be a fashion designer!" she exclaimed. "And the second choice would be a translator – that could be interesting, too."
Soon afterwards, Evie let out a shriek of excitement which attracted a glare from Mrs Skelton.
"Sorry," she said, before she continued more quietly: "My results say that I should be a sports journalist! That really does sound like my perfect job."
The whole class had to wait for Holly to finish her test. She bit her lip and stared upwards, deep in thought, every time she had to answer a new question. Everyone was starting to talk loudly while they waited. In the meantime, Mrs Skelton's voice was getting louder and louder while she tried to calm everybody down.
"Finally, I've answered all those hard questions!" Holly eventually exclaimed.
"And...?" asked Nina. "What's the result?"
"Oh, yes, the result. It said I should be a writer, or a poet, or maybe an artist."

ÜBUNG 10: Career test. Finde heraus, welcher Beruf zu dir passen würde!

1. Which subjects do you enjoy most at school?
   a) ❑ Maths and science.
   b) ❑ Creative subjects, such as art and music.
   c) ❑ Foreign languages.

2. Imagine your life ten years from now. What is your dream situation?
   a) ❑ I have a successful job that helps other people.
   b) ❑ I have a relaxed lifestyle and my work is fun.
   c) ❑ I live in a different country and my life is exciting.

3. What is your nightmare situation?
   a) ❑ I feel like I am wasting all my skills.
   b) ❑ I have money, but there is no meaning in my life.
   c) ❑ I have a boring job in a boring town and there is no adventure in my life.

4. What would make you feel most proud?
   a) ❑ Discovering the cure for a disease.
   b) ❑ Having one of my paintings shown in a famous gallery.
   c) ❑ Learning to speak five languages perfectly.

"Well done, everyone," said Mrs Skelton. "I think we're all finished now."

She looked pointedly at Holly. "You will need to use what you have just learned to help you during the next part of the class. So please pay attention, all of you."

Holly looked nervous. She dreaded having to make any more difficult decisions.

"As you should already know, you will all be doing your work experience soon," said Mrs Skelton. "Unless you want to organize your own, you will need to write down your top three job choices to help the school to find the right choice for you."

She handed out paper so that everyone could write down their choices.

Emily put up her hand to talk to the teacher. She had already organized her own work experience at the beginning of the summer holidays. She was going to be an assistant at an important laboratory. Of course, she had also brought in all the official documents and letters to show to Mrs Skelton.

Nina wrote down her choices quickly. They were all linked to fashion. Holly was also surprisingly quick

pointedly	demonstrativ, bewusst
to dread sth.	etw. fürchten
work experience	*hier:* Berufspraktikum
laboratory	Labor

to complete her list. She was tired of making choices and had simply written the top three results that the test had given her earlier.
Evie had already handed back her paper before the others had even begun to write. Right at the top of the sheet, she had written "sports journalist" in large letters.

ÜBUNG 11: Verb forms. Unterstreiche die richtige Verbform!

1. Emily is going to be/is an assistant at a laboratory.
2. Everyone was starting to talk loudly while they waited/have waited.
3. Olly saw/was seeing Evie in the garden and has gone/went over to her.
4. Nina and Holly were/have been worried when they were seeing/saw the damp piece of paper.
5. Today, Nina has written/wrote down her choices quickly.
6. After Evie started/had started to answer the questions, she found/was finding them interesting.

Much to her surprise, Evie had enjoyed her first day back at school. Yet in spite of her good mood, she still felt that something was missing.

When the girls' conversation turned to boys on their walk home, Evie remembered how much fun she had had with Connor. The memory suddenly made her feel sad.

"I still can't believe that I've ruined my chance of a great relationship," she sighed.

The other girls knew exactly what she meant but were not sure how to make her feel better.

"I'm sure you'll meet someone else soon," said Nina after a pause. "There are plenty of other great guys for you to get to know... like Will, for example. He has an amazing body!"

to be tired of sth.	genug von etw. haben
much to her surprise	zu ihrer großen Überraschung
plenty	jede Menge
to bang	schlagen, knallen
gig	Popkonzert, Auftritt

"But I'm not interested in Will, or his amazing body," Evie replied. "I've never felt the same about anybody else as I do about Connor. Not even when I had a crush on Nick... Oh, I'm so stupid!" She banged her hand against her head in frustration.

Emily put her arm around Evie and told her that things would be alright in the end.

"And anyway," she said, "you'll soon be having so much fun that you'll forget all about it. We're going to that gig next week, remember? There's no way that won't cheer you up! We've been looking forward to it for months!"

"I suppose you're right," Evie agreed.

However, inside she felt that forgetting about Connor was the last thing she wanted to do right now. As she returned home, she hoped that somehow she would be given a second chance at love.

ÜBUNG 12: Odd one out! Welches Wort ist das „schwarze Schaf"?

1. relationship, friendship, falling in love, boyfriend
2. miserable, depressed, moody, cheerful
3. green, red, apple, orange
4. said, think, run, study
5. library, lake, school, museum

3

When It Rains, It Pours

3

Glücklicherweise wird Evie heute ein wenig von ihren tristen Gedanken abgelenkt, denn in der Schule werden die Praktikumsplätze vergeben. Und Evie bekommt tatsächlich einen Platz in der Sportredaktion einer Zeitung! Wenigstens etwas, worüber sie sich freuen kann.
Und dann ist da ja auch noch das Konzert, zu dem die Freundinnen am nächsten Tag gehen. Während des Konzerts ist Evie einfach nur happy, doch dann geschieht etwas völlig Unerwartetes: Mitten in der Menge glaubt sie plötzlich Connor zu entdecken!

One week later, Mrs Skelton told the class that their work experience details had been decided. The girls waited anxiously to hear which jobs they would be doing during their two-week placements.
The teacher handed everyone a letter, telling each pupil where they would spend the two weeks. They all opened their envelopes quickly. Evie had been wondering about her placement all week. She did not dare to hope that she would really be able to try out being a sports journalist. Her older brothers, who had already done their

work experience, had told her that most of the placements were in shops, not at newspaper offices.

Suddenly, Nina shouted: "I'm going to be working at Supershop! It'll be fantastic being surrounded by so many nice clothes all day... I hope I get a staff discount!"

When it rains, it pours.	Ein Unglück kommt selten allein.
anxiously	*hier:* ungeduldig
placement	(Praktikums-)Platz
to dare	wagen
staff discount	Mitarbeiterrabatt
ϟ loads of	jede Menge
cheerful	fröhlich, aufgekratzt
unlike	anders als

The others congratulated both Nina and Holly, who had just found out that she would be working in an art shop. Emily already knew what she would be doing, because she had organized it weeks ago. Evie was pleased for her friends, but hoped that she would not be working in a shop as well.

"Wow! I'm going to be working with the top sports journalist at a local newspaper!" she gasped. "I can't believe it!"

"That's fantastic," Emily said. "I told you there was loads of stuff for you to look forward to! You'll be doing your dream job soon, and the gig is tomorrow, too!"

Evie thought about Emily's words. It was true that she did have many reasons to be excited and cheerful. Her work experience would be unlike anything that she had ever done before, and it might help her to discover her perfect job. And the concert would surely be great fun – all four of them would be going to watch one of their favourite

to persuade sb.	jmd. überzeugen
to darken	verdüstern, verfinstern
mark	Fleck, Mal
shred of hope	Fünkchen Hoffnung
to distract	ablenken
stage	Bühne

singers, Jerome Carey, sing live in the city nearby. Even Emily, who was often not allowed to stay out late or join the others on trips, had managed to persuade her parents to let her go with the other girls. However, one thing still darkened Evie's mood. She still kept the piece of paper with Connor's blurred telephone number by her bed and looked at it every morning, hoping for an answer. But every morning, she could only see the messy blue mark on the page. As she stared at the ugly mark, she felt the last shreds of hope disappear. All that was left was one thought: I'll never see Connor again!

The next day, all that Holly, Nina and Emily could talk about was the concert. Even Evie's feelings about Connor could not stop her from being a bit excited, too. She enjoyed the long conversations with her friends about favourite songs and music videos, because they distracted her from her sad thoughts.

By the time school had finally finished, the girls could not wait any longer. They hurried home to change out of their school uniforms and into more stylish outfits.

An hour later, they met at the railway station where they would catch the train to the arena.

ÜBUNG 13: Adjective or adverb? Setze die richtige Form ein!

1. The girls waited *(anxious)* .... until Mrs Skelton handed out the letters.
2. Everyone opened their envelopes *(quick)* ....
3. Emily's parents are very *(strict)* ....
4. Nina thinks it will be *(fantastic)* .... to work in a *(nice)* .... shop all day.
5. She did have many reasons to be *(cheerful)* ...., thought Evie *(cheerful)* ....
6. The girls hurried home to *(quick)* .... change into *(stylish)* .... outfits.

"We have to make sure we get as close to the stage as possible," Emily said as the train left the station and carried them towards the city.

Holly agreed with her. "I want to be able to see Jerome's face clearly and imagine that he's singing the songs just for me..." She closed her eyes and smiled, as though she were imagining it at that very moment.

"We should queue up as soon as we get there, so we can be sure to get a place at the front," Nina said.

at that very moment	genau in diesem Moment
to queue (up)	sich anstellen, Schlange stehen
to wind around	laufen um, sich winden um
exhilaration	überschwängliche Freude
to scream	schreien, kreischen
to squeeze	drücken
swaying crowd	sich wiegende Menge

Everyone thought that this was a good idea. After a short walk from the city railway station to the arena, the four girls joined the queue and waited for what seemed like a long time. However, they soon felt glad that they had arrived so early, because the line of people waiting grew longer and longer. A short while later, the queue was already winding around the outside of the building. Luckily, they had brought some food and magazines and were certainly not bored while they waited. It was so exciting to be together in the big city, away from parents and teachers.

Eventually, it was time to enter the arena. The girls ran to the stage as soon as they could. Evie got to the front and smiled: she would have a perfect view of the concert. The space around the girls filled quickly until they were pushed closer and closer together, but they did not mind at all. As hundreds and hundreds of other young people poured through the doors, the whole arena was filled with a feeling of shared exhilaration. Evie could not think of anywhere she would rather be.

Suddenly, the stage was lit up with bright colours. A few moments later, Jerome Carey came onto the stage and Evie's ears were hit by the sound of hundreds of people screaming. She squeezed Emily's hand and looked at her with wide, excited eyes. Her usually quiet friend was screaming wildly.

The first song was one of Evie's favourites and she started dancing with her arms in the air and a huge smile on her face. Everybody else in the arena seemed to be dancing, too. Evie loved being in the centre of the swaying crowd.

She was having such a wonderful time with her friends that an hour went by very quickly. Evie was surprised and disappointed when the music stopped and the singer left the stage.

"Oh no! That can't be the end, can it?"

"No, don't worry," Nina replied. "It just means that it's time for the encore."

Nina was right. The crowd continued to cheer and after a minute or so, Jerome returned to the stage with his guitar. Evie cheered even louder.

The third song of the encore was one of the singer's most popular songs. Evie recognized the song immediately. The whole crowd started to sing along, and many people, including Evie, were dancing and jumping up and down.

Suddenly, as she jumped and moved her head in time with the music, something caught her eye. Something that shocked her so much that the sound of the song she loved so much faded into background noise.

encore	Zugabe
in time with the music	im Takt der Musik
to catch sb.'s eye	jmd. auffallen
to fade	schwinden, verblassen
background noise	Hintergrund-rauschen
split second	Sekunden-bruchteil

At the other side of the stage, in the middle of the dancing crowd, she thought she saw Connor!

Everything seemed to slow down and all the noise of the crowd fell silent for a split second when Evie saw Connor appear. He was dancing at the other side of the stage close to two other people. Only a moment later, the two people moved nearer to each other again and Connor's face was lost in the crowd.

Evie stood completely still, while everyone around her moved. She opened her mouth in shock and tried to work out what to do. She carried on looking, but she did not see Connor again: there were too many people between them. She decided that she would have to go over and look for him.

ÜBUNG 14: Match-up. Verbinde die Gegensatzpaare!

1. wildly	silence
2. enter	booing
3. huge	dark
4. front	forever
5. bright	tiny
6. cheering	leave
7. noise	calmly
8. split second	back

Moving through the crowd was very difficult, because everybody was dancing wildly to the song and there was so little space. But in spite of the commotion, Evie moved as quickly as she could, because she could not let herself miss her one chance to see Connor again. Even when people stood on her feet and accidentally hit her arms as they jumped, she kept moving forward. Eventually, she reached the other side of the stage, where she thought Connor had been. She looked all around her, but still she could not find him.

The song was reaching its end and the music had become louder and more energetic. Surrounded by so many people, a lot of noise and flashing lights, Evie suddenly felt confused and lost – not only could she not find Connor, but now she no longer knew where her friends were, either. She did not know what to do. By now she was beginning to feel a little scared.

Moments later, the song ended and the whole crowd cheered and clapped, as the singer left the stage. Evie also clapped, but did not even see him go. She was too busy looking around for Connor to look at the stage.

The crowd started to move again, but this time everybody moved towards the exit doors. Again, Evie stood still, trying to find a familiar face in the commotion. The arena emptied slowly until eventually there was almost nobody left by the stage except her. Evie's heart was heavy with disappointment: she had been so close to Connor but had lost him once again.

At that moment, her mobile phone beeped. It was a text message from Emily, telling Evie that her three friends were waiting for her outside. Sadly, Evie accepted that it was time to go home, and that her chance of finding Connor was lost. She walked towards the exit doors to meet her friends outside. On the way, she continued to look around but without any real hope of finding Connor.

commotion	Tumult, Gedränge
energetic	schwungvoll, energisch
flashing	blinkend, aufleuchtend
not only... but...	nicht nur ..., sondern (auch) ...
refreshing	erfrischend
puddle	Pfütze
to splash	spritzen
into the distance	*hier:* davon, weg

Then she realized: she had only seen him for a split second, not really long enough to be sure of recognizing someone properly. What's more, she had been thinking about Connor so much lately that she could easily have imagined that it was him. She had probably seen somebody else who looked a bit like him.

Evie walked out into the rainy night. Bright city lights and the sound of busy traffic met her outside the arena. She enjoyed the refreshing rain on her hot skin, but she did not enjoy what happened next.

A car drove through a puddle right in front of her, splashing muddy water all over her brand new trousers and her favourite top. She looked up angrily at the car that was now driving away into the distance and felt like shouting.

ÜBUNG 15: Reading comprehension. Beantworte die Fragen zum Text!

1. How do the girls get to the concert?

....

2. Why are the girls glad to be at the arena early?

....

3. Why is it difficult for Evie to move through the crowd?

....

....

4. Why does Evie suddenly feel confused and lost?

....

....

5. Why does Emily's text message make Evie feel even worse?

....

....

6. What makes Evie think that she may not have seen Connor after all?

....

Suddenly Evie saw a boy in the back of another car as it drove past her – a boy with quite long, blond hair and a dimple on his left cheek. This time, she had a little longer to look at him, and she felt sure that it could not be anyone else but Connor. Without thinking, Evie called out his name as loudly as she could and started to run after the car. She did not even think about how she must have looked, wet and muddy and shouting after him as the car drove away from her. But her shouting did not help at all, because he just carried on looking ahead without seeing the strange figure calling after him. Soon the car disappeared into the distance just like the other one, and Evie was left alone and soaking wet outside the arena.

soaking wet klatschnass

This time, it was all too much for her. She started to cry and could not stop again. She sat down at the side of the road as tears rolled down her face. The rain, which was falling even more heavily than before, mixed with her tears.

"Evie!" cried a voice behind her. "There you are! We were so worried when you didn't come to find us!"

"What are you doing out here?" asked another voice. "You're all wet and you must be freezing!"

Evie looked around. She saw her friends coming towards her with worried expressions. Emily gave Evie her hand to help her up, and Evie stood up slowly.

"What on earth happened?" Emily asked gently.

Evie looked at her sadly. "I saw Connor."

"What? How?" asked Holly.

Evie shrugged her shoulders. "He was at the concert. He lives near here, too."

"So what happened?" asked Nina. "Why are you outside on your own in the rain?"

Evie explained everything that had happened while they walked away from the arena towards the car park. Emily's father had come to take the girls home by car because her parents had not wanted them to take the train so late at night.

Evie did not want to talk about Connor in front of Emily's father and therefore did not speak on the journey home. Instead, she cried a few silent tears while Emily held her hand.

to freeze	(er)frieren
to shrug one's shoulders	die Schultern zucken
support	Unterstützung
to fall through	ins Wasser fallen
to cancel	streichen, absagen

ÜBUNG 16: Hidden words. Finde im Suchrätsel zehn Wörter aus dem Text!

A	G	C	O	F	R	E	E	Z	I	N	G
X	S	O	A	K	I	N	G	C	P	K	D
F	U	N	U	A	J	P	C	T	C	Z	J
E	Y	C	S	H	O	U	T	F	A	U	O
N	E	E	H	I	Z	D	K	X	T	P	U
C	R	R	U	M	U	D	D	Y	K	I	R
O	O	T	H	P	R	L	S	H	O	B	N
R	N	G	D	L	T	E	A	R	S	L	E
E	B	O	V	E	Q	U	B	A	K	U	Y
N	C	H	N	J	A	R	S	I	R	O	E
F	B	A	R	H	Z	E	T	N	A	L	P

The next day was a Saturday, so Evie decided to invite her friends over to her house. She was still feeling terrible, and thought that they were the only people who would be able to cheer her up. However, she did not realize that one of her friends would need her support as well.
Nina and Holly had already arrived by the time Emily knocked on the door. She came in, looking stressed and upset.
"My work experience has fallen through!" Emily told them as soon as she entered the sitting room. "I can't believe it, after how hard I worked to organize it."
"They can't just cancel it now, can they?" asked Evie. "It's supposed to start in a week!"

"Well, I guess they can," Emily replied, "because they just have. The woman who I was going to be working with at the laboratory called me this morning. She told me that they have to do some important tests over the next month and will be too busy to give me any training. She didn't even say sorry!"
"That's terrible," said Holly. "Can't they let you work there without training?"
"No, because they say that it wouldn't be safe."
"So what are you going to do?" asked Nina.
"I'll have to see if there are any placements left. But it's so late that all the good ones are probably gone by now." Emily looked very upset.
Evie knew that Emily took her studies seriously, but secretly she could not find much sympathy for her at the moment. She had invited everyone over because of her own problems, not to hear about Emily's. Emily was worried about nothing anyway, she thought to herself. While Holly and Nina comforted Emily, Evie did not say anything. Emily cares more about school than she does about boys, she thought spitefully.
Emily changed the subject. "Sorry, Evie," she said, "I didn't mean to come here just to moan – I know you must be really upset about last night. Why don't you tell us again how it all happened?"
Evie suddenly felt bad about everything that she had thought about Emily before. She remembered that even if Emily did put school before boys, she would always put her friends first.

training	Ausbildung, Schulung
sympathy	Mitgefühl
to comfort sb.	jmd. trösten
spitefully	gehässig
to moan	jammern, klagen
to put school before boys	die Schule wichtiger nehmen als Jungs

Evie told them the whole story of what had happened, from seeing Connor in the crowd to running after the car in the rain, shouting his name.

When she had finished, Emily hugged her. "That must have been so upsetting," she said. "But maybe it's a good sign that fate wants to bring the two of you together again, like I said."

"If it was fate, then why did Connor leave without even recognizing me?" Evie asked. "That just doesn't make sense."

Emily thought about it and shrugged her shoulders.

"I don't know, but there has to be a reason for all this happening," she said. "It doesn't seem fair – you've been so upset about Connor anyway without being reminded of it in such a horrible way."

"When it rains, it pours, I guess," Evie said. "And now you've lost your work experience, too. I wonder what the next bad thing to happen to us will be."

The following Monday, the first thing Emily did at school was to tell Mrs Skelton about her cancelled work experience. The teacher told her that she would know by the end of the school day whether the school could find a new placement for her. Emily waited anxiously all morning and afternoon. After the last lesson, she went to see Mrs Skelton

at such short notice	so kurzfristig
to be amazed that...	erstaunt sein, dass ...

to find out what, if anything, the school had been able to find for her.

"The good news is that there is one placement left. It's a job in a supermarket," Mrs Skelton told her. She saw the disappointment in Emily's green eyes and added, "I know this is not what you wanted, but give it a chance. Work is so very different from school – it can be surprising."

Emily could not see how a job in a supermarket could be surprising. But it was too late to find anything else. Feeling miserable, she thanked the teacher for her help and left.

ÜBUNG 17: True or false? Kreuze die richtigen Aussagen an!

1. Emily seemed fine when she arrived at Evie's house. ❑
2. Emily's work experience had been cancelled because the laboratory was too busy. ❑
3. Emily was not worried about finding another placement. ❑
4. At first, Evie felt really sorry for Emily. ❑
5. Emily felt sorry for Evie, so she changed the subject to talk about Connor. ❑

"A supermarket?" Evie asked in a shocked voice. She had waited for Emily before walking home.
"That's right," said Emily. "But I didn't really think I'd get anything better at such short notice."
"But it's not your fault!" said Evie. This time she really did feel a lot of sympathy for her best friend. "You were the only person who organized their work experience months early. It shouldn't be you who has to take the placement that nobody else wanted!"
"Oh well," Emily sighed. "Sometimes things just happen that way."
Evie was amazed that Emily could accept her situation so easily. She wished that she could do the same, but no matter how hard she tried, she simply could not forget the boy who had kissed her in the rain.

ÜBUNG 18: Unscramble the excuses! Bilde sinnvolle Entschuldigungen mit den durcheinander geratenen Satzteilen!

1. because – I'm late – a lot of traffic – there was

....

....

2. my dog – homework – I'm – ate – my – sorry

....

....

3. already knew – you – I thought

....

....

4. I've – I haven't – ill – because – done it – been

....

....

5. I didn't know – kissed him – you fancied – I – him – when

....

....

4

Weathering the Storm

4

Heute ist Evies erster Praktikumstag bei der Zeitung. Zu dumm nur, dass sie nicht daran gedacht hat, den Wecker früher zu stellen! Sie kommt zu spät und überhaupt verläuft der Tag nicht sehr erfreulich – Evie ist verunsichert und ihre Vorgesetzte Carla überlässt ihr nur uninteressante Aufgaben. Außerdem muss Evie oft an Connor denken. Sie ist total niedergeschlagen. Doch dann bekommt Evie endlich ihre große Chance: Sie darf zu einem Fußballmatch, um einen Artikel darüber zu schreiben! Aufgeregt macht Evie sich an die Vorbereitung …

Evie woke up to find that the sun was shining through the window and filling the whole room with warm light. Still sleepy, she tried to move away from the brightness and immediately fell out of her bed and onto the hard floor. "Ow!" she said loudly, as she tried to lift herself up. Oh well, she thought, at least I'm out of bed already. Usually, Evie struggled to get up in time for school. Her parents often had to help by shouting at her several times to wake her up before Evie would eventually drag herself out of bed.
Sure enough, at that moment, Evie's mother

came through the door, ready to wake Evie.
"TIME TO WAKE UP – oh," she said, surprised to find her daughter standing next to her bed rather than still lying in it. "You must be excited about your work experience!"
Work experience, Evie thought, looking at the clock. Didn't she have to get up earlier than usual to catch the bus to the newspaper office? She had forgotten to change the alarm time, and the time on the alarm clock now read 07:59. A moment later, it changed to 08:00, and the alarm started to make a loud and annoying sound.

to weather the storm	eine Sache (gut) überstehen
to lift oneself up	aufstehen, sich aufrappeln
to struggle	Mühe haben, kämpfen
to drag	schleppen, schlurfen
⚡ sure enough	tatsächlich, wirklich
exasperated	aufgebracht, verärgert

"Oh no! I'm going to be late on my first day!" she cried.
"But you're up earlier than usual, Evie," her mother told her. "You have nothing to worry about."
"You don't understand! The office is a long way away – I was supposed to get up half an hour ago."
Her mother looked a bit confused. "Oh, I thought you were going into school first."
Evie replied in an exasperated voice. "Why would I go to – oh never mind, Mum! I need to get ready, right now!"

She closed the door after her mother had left the room and quickly started to put her clothes on. There was no time for a shower.
Ten minutes later, she ran out of the house and down into town to catch the bus. Her messy red hair was still unbrushed and she had buttoned up her blouse wrongly so that one side ended up longer than the other. But even though Evie ran as fast as she could, she still arrived just in time to see the bus drive away in front of her. Why does everything keep going wrong, she thought in frustration.
Luckily, she only had to wait fifteen minutes for the next bus, but Evie knew that she would still be late for work. She anxiously thought about what to say to Carla Anderson, the woman she was going to be working with at the newspaper.

unbrushed	ungebürstet
to button up	zuknöpfen
conscious	bewusst
on time	pünktlich
She wished that the ground would swallow her up.	Sie wünschte, sie würde im Boden versinken.

Nervously, Evie walked into the office of The Post, suddenly feeling conscious of her messy hair and quickly chosen clothes. In front of her, a woman with long, curly hair was talking to an older man.
"I told you," said the woman in a loud voice. "It was a mistake to agree to this work experience thing. The girl can't even make it to work on time on her first day – how is she going to do anything useful around here?"

ÜBUNG 19: Prepositions. Vervollständige die Sätze mit den folgenden Präpositionen!

out of | *for* | *up* | *in* | *on* | *at* | *to* | *with*

1. Evie was worried that she would be late .... work.
2. Evie usually struggled to get .... bed in time for school.
3. Evie put her clothes .... wrongly, because she was .... a hurry.
4. .... the newspaper, Evie was working .... Carla Anderson.
5. She ran .... the bus stop.
6. On Monday morning, Evie was .... earlier than usual.

Before the man could reply, he noticed Evie standing behind them and they both turned around to look at her. Evie wished that the ground would swallow her up. She did not know what she should say to make this horrible and unfamiliar situation any better, so she simply apologized for her lateness.

greying hair	graumeliertes Haar
frosty	frostig
whereas	wohingegen, während

"Don't worry about it," said the man.

Compared to the woman, who looked quite unfriendly, he seemed kind. He had large, interested eyes and greying hair. He introduced himself as Ian.

The woman turned to Evie and held out her hand.

"Hi, I'm Carla," she said in a frosty tone. "You must be the work experience girl."

Ian explained that Carla was the newspaper's top sports journalist, whereas he was the editor. Evie would spend

the next two weeks assisting Carla. And if she did well, she would be given the chance to write her own article for the newspaper at the end of the placement.

Although the thought of working closely with Carla for two whole weeks made Evie's heart sink, she was very excited when she heard that her writing might end up in the newspaper. She wanted to work hard and make the most of her opportunity.

But when Carla started to explain what Evie would be helping her with, it did not sound at all like hard work. Evie had to do a bit of filing, make cups of tea and answer the telephone.

editor	Redakteur
sb.'s heart sinks	jmd. rutscht das Herz in die Hose
opportunity	Chance, Gelegenheit
filing	Akten ablegen, Ablage

She was going to have to start immediately, because the phone rang in the middle of their conversation.

"Well go on, answer it then," said Carla impatiently.

Evie picked up the phone, but as soon as she put it to her ear, she realized that she was not sure what she was supposed to say – she was only used to answering the phone to her friends and family.

"Uh, hello," she said.

There was a pause.

Evie was unsure about what to say next, so she simply asked: "What is it you want?"

Carla's eyes widened in shock. After the phone call had ended, she told Evie never to answer the phone in that way again. "You don't say 'hello, what is it you want'!" she explained. "You say 'good morning, you're speaking to Evie at The Post. How may I help you?'"

Evie felt so stupid. She had such easy tasks to carry out, but even this simple thing had been too much for her. She went to make tea for the rest of the office. She wondered whether Carla was right and the placement had all been a big mistake.

ÜBUNG 20: Formal or informal? Kreuze die Ausdrücke an, die du nicht nur unter Freunden sondern auch gegenüber Erwachsenen benutzen kannst!

1. How may I help you? ❑
2. See ya later. ❑
3. Do you need a hand? ❑
4. How are you? ❑
5. Hiya. ❑
6. How's it going? ❑
7. No way! ❑
8. Goodbye. ❑

The week went by without much enjoyment for Evie. Every day, she would make the journey to the office in a miserable mood, spend the day feeling useless and then leave in an even worse mood than when she had started.

to widen in shock	sich vor Schreck weiten
to carry out a task	eine Aufgabe erledigen
enjoyment	Vergnügen, Spaß
all of a sudden	plötzlich, auf einmal
determined	entschlossen
career	Karriere, Laufbahn

Most of the people in her office seemed nice, but they had a lot of work to do, so they did not often stop to talk to her. Evie felt very young all of a sudden. Everybody else in the office knew exactly what they were doing and sounded so clever when they spoke. But Evie still seemed to get even the simplest things wrong.

Each day at work was hard, but Evie tried to weather the storm by paying attention to what the journalists were doing. She knew that this was the only way she would get an idea of the job, because Carla was no help. On the contrary, she seemed determined to stop Evie from getting any experience that could possibly be useful for a career as a journalist.

Evie also tried to concentrate on the good things that she could do when she was not at work. Each day she chose something that she enjoyed, like going swimming, or watching a film. That way she had the evenings to look forward to and her working days did not seem quite so bad.

It also stopped her from thinking about Connor, who was always somewhere in the back of her mind during those days. She would find herself daydreaming about him while she was in the middle of doing her office tasks and had to force herself to concentrate on her work.

to force oneself	sich zwingen
to criticize	kritisieren
to trust sb. to do sth.	jmd. zutrauen, etw. zu tun
essay	Aufsatz
customer	Kunde
disastrous	katastrophal
ϟ wicked	abgefahren, super
ϟ Guess what!	Stellt euch vor!

On Thursday Evie did not have to think hard to find something to look forward to, because she and her friends had already arranged to go out for pizza. That evening, the four girls met at Pizza Palace at seven o'clock.

Evie had already told her friends how unhappy she was at The Post, but they were still surprised to see her looking so miserable. Evie explained to them that Carla criticized everything she did and how she was not trusted to do any more than make tea for the others.

"I'll never get to write an article for the newspaper like this," she sighed. "But anyway, let's talk about something more cheerful. I'm sure the rest of you have been having a great time."

"I have," Nina replied. "It's been fun doing something other than school work for a change. What I like most is to get home knowing that there's no homework to do or lessons to prepare for."

Even Evie could agree with that. She loved having her evenings all to herself rather than spending them struggling over maths homework or writing essays.

"I like helping the customers, too," Holly said, talking about her work in an art shop. "Although sometimes I'm not sure if I'm doing it right."

Evie knew what she meant, but was too embarrassed to tell the others about her disastrous first phone call at the beginning of the week. Instead, she asked Emily whether the supermarket job was any better than she had expected.

"Well, yes," Emily replied. "It's been really good."

"Really?" asked Nina. "I thought you were upset about having to work there."

"I was, but it's been much better than I thought. There are some great people working there and they make everything so much fun. It's been wicked!"

The others were surprised. Emily did not normally use slang words, and she was certainly not the type of person they would have expected to enjoy working in a supermarket. Evie guessed that there was something that her friend was not telling them. But Nina soon changed the subject, so, for now, Evie forgot all about the idea.

"Oh, and guess what!" Nina said happily. "They've given me some free clothes! Everyone has to wear Supershop clothes

at all times, so they told me that I could pick any outfit from the shop and that I can keep it when I leave!"
Emily and Holly both told her how lucky she was. Then they told stories about their own experiences at work. Evie listened to them with mixed feelings. One part of her was happy that everyone was having such a great time, but the other felt left out and disappointed. A week ago she had thought that her placement was by far the best out of all of them, but now she felt jealous of the other girls. The stories they shared only reminded her of what she herself was missing out on.
Evie was sure that they did not want to hear her stories. And she guessed that they must be sick of hearing about Connor by now, too, so she stayed unusually quiet.

ÜBUNG 21: Odd one out! Welches Wort ist das „schwarze Schaf"?

1. office, supermarket, shop, store
2. ball, book, team, goal
3. jealous, disastrous, sickening, comforting
4. T-shirt, surfboard, skirt, trousers
5. guess, realize, exclaim, think
6. fashion, newspaper, editor, journalist

The next day started badly. When Evie arrived at work, everybody in the office already seemed busy. Everyone was working on a big news story, and a lot of the journalists looked stressed and tired. Many had come into work hours before to try and get the work done.

Evie tried to be helpful, but the busy atmosphere just made her feel in the way. Carla was at a tennis match, so Evie had nothing to do. Nobody asked her for help, because their work was too difficult for her.

Evie usually ate her lunch in a park right next to the office, but that day she felt like she wanted to be further away. So she decided to surprise Emily by meeting her at the supermarket where she was working, which was only a short walk away.

The front of the supermarket was almost completely made of glass. As Evie turned the corner and walked towards the shop, she recognized Emily's long, black hair through the glass from a long way away. Emily seemed to be trying to put some food on the shelves, but every time she put something away, a tall, dark-haired boy pulled it back down and dropped it into Emily's lap. Evie did not understand: was her friend being bullied?

with mixed feelings	mit gemischten Gefühlen
to feel left out	sich ausgeschlossen fühlen
jealous	eifersüchtig
to miss out on sth.	etw. verpassen
ϟ to feel in the way	sich fehl am Platz vorkommen
shelf	Regal
lap	Schoß
to bully	drangsalieren, mobben

As she walked closer to the shop window, Evie felt hot anger rising up inside her. But then she noticed something strange: Emily was smiling happily and hitting the boy on the arm.
Evie went into the supermarket and started walking towards Emily, who now had her back towards her. Emily had not seen her. She and the boy were talking to each other and Evie was close enough to hear some of what they were saying.
"You should come, too," the dark-haired boy said with a smile. "It's going to be wicked."

anger	Wut
to blush	erröten
to mess around	herumalbern
crush	Schwarm
to spread	sich ausbreiten
instantly	augenblicklich, sofort

ÜBUNG 22: Match-up. Welche Wörter passen inhaltlich zusammen?

1. decide	unexpectedly
2. strange	puzzled
3. suddenly	choose
4. confused	joy
5. rage	exhausted
6. tired	anger
7. happiness	odd

"What was going on just then?" asked Evie. Emily had left the shop quickly once she had seen her friend arrive. Now, the two of them were sitting in a quiet café to have their lunch. Emily blushed. "That was Josh. We were just messing around."

Evie could not believe that she had not guessed before: of course, Emily had a crush! *That* was why she was enjoying work so much.

"Oh, Emily," said Evie. "I will never understand why you don't just tell us about your crushes. It's not going to come as a shock to any of us that you like a boy!"

"I know, but it will probably all be over when we go back to school."

"It didn't look that way," said Evie. "I think he likes you, too. And didn't he invite you somewhere tonight?"

Suddenly, Emily's expression changed completely. A smile spread instantly across her face as she explained what Josh had said.

"He's invited some friends over tonight and he told me that I should come, too. I'm not sure though, because I don't know any of his friends."

relief	Erleichterung
far too quickly	viel zu schnell
to trudge	trotten, sich schleppen

"Don't be silly!" Evie said loudly. "OF COURSE you're going to go!" Emily eventually agreed. A few hours later, Evie received a text message from her. Emily was having a great evening with Josh, and she thought that he was flirting with her.
Holly smiled. If even Emily could tell that Josh was flirting with her, then he must really like her.

To Evie's relief, the weekend finally arrived. On Saturday, she went to football practice as usual and on Sunday, she went shopping with the other girls. The weekend seemed to pass far too quickly and, once again, it was time to go back to the job she hated so much.
On Monday morning, Evie trudged into the office with her head down and the corners of her mouth turned in the same direction. She was just about to ask everyone if they wanted a cup of tea, when Ian, the editor, came to talk to her.
"Good morning, Evie," he said in a kind voice. "How did your first week go?"
Evie tried to lie and tell him that it had gone well, but she could not force her mouth to speak the words, or to widen into a smile.

ÜBUNG 23: Does he fancy you? Finde heraus ob dein Schwarm auch in dich verknallt ist!

1. How does he act when he talks to you?
   a) ❑ He seems a bit nervous, as if he is trying to impress me. *(10 points)*
   b) ❑ He smiles a lot and teases me sometimes. *(7 points)*
   c) ❑ We haven't really spoken before, apart from saying "hi" once. *(0 points)*

2. Does he ever look at you from across the room?
   a) ❑ No, I have never noticed that. *(0 points)*
   b) ❑ Yes, often. *(10 points)*
   c) ❑ Sometimes, but I wonder if it is because I look at him so often myself. *(5 points)*

3. Does he have a girlfriend or a crush?
   a) ❑ He says he fancies somebody, but won't tell me who it is. *(10 points)*
   b) ❑ Yes, he has a girlfriend. *(0 points)*
   c) ❑ I think he has a crush on someone else. *(3 points)*

4. Has he ever told you that he thinks he fancies you?
   a) ❑ No. *(0 points)*
   b) ❑ Yes, but he is not sure. *(5 points)*
   c) ❑ Yes, my friends tease me about it all the time! *(10 points)*

Your score: ____________

"It's been... fine," Evie managed to say.
"What have you been writing about?" Ian asked her.
Surprised, Evie looked up at him. "So far, I haven't been asked to do any writing," she replied honestly.

concerned	besorgt
premier league	Erste Liga
versus	gegen
pang	Stich, Anfall
to prove	beweisen

Ian looked concerned. "Wait a moment, Evie," he said, before disappearing into Carla's office.
A short while later, Ian returned with Carla. Ian spoke first. "We have both decided that it's important that you get some real experience of writing about sport while you're here. So Carla is going to take you to a premier league football match this Wednesday."
Evie's eyes lit up with excitement. A free ticket to a premier league match was the best thing that she could have been given – much better than Nina's free outfit, she thought.
"It's Liverpool versus Chelsea," Ian continued.
This was even better news for Evie, because that was one of the most important matches of the year. However, she felt a sudden pang of sadness when she remembered that Liverpool was Connor's favourite football team – just one of the many things that still reminded her of him. She tried to put that feeling to the back of her mind and continued listening to Ian.
"It will be lots of fun," he said. "But remember that there's also a serious reason why you are there. Your job is to take

notes for the article that you will write when you get back. So, don't have too much fun and remember to work hard!"
Evie saw that Carla was rolling her eyes and looking at her watch. She thought that with Carla around, having too much fun would not be a problem.
In spite of this, Evie felt happy about her work experience for the first time since it had begun. She hoped that she would finally be able to prove to Carla that she was not useless after all.

ÜBUNG 24: Fill in the blanks to find the word.

1. Emily went on ... to Florida
   .... ▮ ....
2. The opposite of a smile .... ▮ ....
3. to act as if you fancy someone .... ▮
4. Connor's favourite football team .... ▮ ....
5. Evie works in an .... ▮ ....
6. Someone who works for a newspaper .... ▮ ....
7. A piece of clothing that covers your legs .... ▮ ....

Lösung: ....

Evie's excitement about the football match filled her with a new enthusiasm for her work. Carla did not ask her to do much, so she tried to help others around the office. On Monday afternoon, she even helped Ian to choose a photograph for the front page of the newspaper. That day she left work with a smile on her face for the first time. She could not wait to tell her family the good news.

"Guess what!" she exclaimed as she ran through the front door and into the living room.

Two of her brothers, Olly and Max, were sitting on the sofa.

"You've just found out that you're adopted?" joked Max cruelly as he looked up.

Evie narrowed her eyes and gave him a look that told him that she did not find his joke very funny.

"Oh, I know," said Olly. "Did you find that boy from the caravan park? What was his name... Connor, right?"

Unlike his brother, Olly had not meant to be cruel, but his words stung Evie much more than Max's had done. Thinking about work had helped her to forget about Connor, at least for a few hours. Now a part of her earlier happiness fell away when she remembered him again. However, she tried to feel excited again while she told Olly and Max about the premier league football match she would be going to in two days.

enthusiasm	Begeisterung
to narrow one's eyes	die Augen zusammenkneifen
to sting sb.	jmd. kränken
statistics	Statistik(en)
to rouse sb. from	*hier:* jmd. reißen aus
research	Recherche
to rest on	liegen auf, ruhen auf

"That's amazing," said Olly. "You're so lucky!"
Max looked jealous but did not say much.
"It's my one chance to show them that I can write a good article and not just make tea," added Evie. "It's really important to me to do well."
"I have loads of football magazines you can look at tonight if you want," Olly told her, trying to be helpful.
"That would be great," Evie said. "I was going to look on the Internet for useful statistics, too. It's a shame that it's not an article about Rangers – then I wouldn't need any help!"
The whole family were Rangers fans. Evie's uncle had even played for Rangers FC for several years when he was younger. Some of Evie's earliest memories were of Rangers matches that her father had taken her to when she was a very young girl.
"That's a good idea," said Olly, rousing Evie from her thoughts. "But you'll do a great job as a sports journalist whatever happens."
He looked at Eve with a kind expression and she instantly felt more relaxed.
"Thanks, Ol," she said. "I'm going to go and start my research for tomorrow."
Evie went upstairs and switched on the computer she shared with her brothers. She wanted to find out everything she could that would help her to write her article. A little later, Olly appeared with some football magazines which he left beside her. After a few hours, he returned to tell her that it was getting late. But he found Evie asleep, with her head resting on one of the open magazines.

The next morning, Evie woke up in her bed without remembering how she had got there. She was still wearing the clothes from the day before.

"Wake up, sleepyhead!" her father shouted through her open door. He came into the room and ruffled her messy hair.

"Last night, Olly found you asleep with your head in a load of football statistics. So I carried you to bed."

"Thank you, Dad," Evie smiled sleepily. "I'll get up now, I promise."

Her father kissed her on the top of her head and left the room.

Evie stretched her arms out wide and yawned. She realized happily that she could remember exactly how many goals each of the top footballers from Liverpool and Chelsea had scored that year. She could also remember many other useful facts that would show Carla how much she knew about football. For once, she could not wait to get to work.

ϟ sleepyhead	Schlafmütze
to ruffle	zerzausen
to promise	versprechen
to stretch	(aus)strecken
to yawn	gähnen
to score a goal	ein Tor schießen

5

On Cloud Nine

5

Am Tag des Spiels ist Evie schon früh in der Redaktion und den ganzen Tag in Hochstimmung. Auch dass Carla während der gesamten Fahrt nicht mit ihr redet, ist ihr egal – schließlich wird ihr Artikel über das Spiel vielleicht sogar in der Zeitung gedruckt!
Im Stadion verfolgt Evie aufgeregt das Spiel und macht sich eifrig Notizen, doch leider ist die Partie ungewöhnlich zäh. Ausgerechnet als dass entscheidende Tor fällt, ist Evie total abgelenkt: Sie hat auf der Videoleinwand einen blonden Jungen erspäht, der ihr sehr bekannt vorkommt … Diesmal darf Connor ihr nicht entwischen!

Evie walked into the office ten minutes early, feeling confident and happy. As she sat down at her desk, the telephone began to ring. She picked it up.
"Good morning, you're speaking to Evie at The Post. How may I help you?" she asked brightly.
"It's Carla," replied a familiar, frosty voice on the other end of the line. "I didn't think you'd be in the office yet. Anyway, please tell Ian that I'm going to be late today. The football match is a long way away, so I'll come and get you

as soon as I get back to the office and we'll leave straight away."

Evie began to reply, but the telephone suddenly started to make a loud noise in her ear. Carla had put the phone down without waiting for an answer.

Never mind, thought Evie. The less time I have to spend talking to Carla, the better.

on cloud nine	auf Wolke sieben
brightly	*hier:* fröhlich, gutgelaunt
never mind	was soll's, egal
the less... the better	je weniger ..., desto besser
to soften	mildern, abschwächen
to suit sb.	jmd. passen, gelegen kommen
notebook	Notizblock
to pass	*hier:* sich zuspielen

Without Carla around, the morning went by quickly. And when she did arrive, the horrible feeling that Evie usually had when she saw her was softened by her excitement about the match. Evie knew that it would only be a few minutes before they left.

The journey to the match passed very quietly. Neither of them spoke much, which seemed to suit both of them. Evie was glad that Carla seemed happy to drive there in silence, because she certainly did not want to talk to her.

They found their seats in silence, too, and waited for the match to begin without speaking to each other. Evie took out her notebook, which already contained notes and useful statistics from the night before.

The match began slowly. Both teams passed the ball around the field, but neither seemed likely to score.

Instead, the defenders seemed to be doing most of the work. Accordingly, it was a long time before Evie had anything interesting to write down in her notebook.

As the match continued, it seemed more and more unlikely that there would be a goal soon. Half-time arrived and, apart from a few notes about the defenders, Evie's notebook was still quite empty. Evie looked up at the sky and noticed heavy grey storm clouds that seemed to mirror her own worried feelings. If nothing exciting happened in the match, she would have no chance of writing an interesting article.

ÜBUNG 25: Short forms. Setze die richtige Kurzform ein!

1. Evie *(was not)* .... late for work.
2. At half-time, the teams still *(had not)* .... scored.
3. "If you *(did not)* .... want to do it, you *(should have)* .... told me."
4. "*(You will)* .... never get good marks if you *(do not)* .... work harder!"
5. "We *(must not)* .... do that again."
6. "*(I would)* .... forgive her if I were you."

The second half of the match began, and Chelsea quickly missed a good chance to score. Evie hoped that a goal would come soon, but before long, the match had returned to the slow rhythm of the first half. She sighed and looked up to the dark sky once again. By now, it was beginning to rain. The footballers carried on playing their slow, defensive game while large, heavy raindrops started to fall. Evie shivered in the autumn cold and wondered what she would write about.

defender	Verteidiger
unlikely	unwahrscheinlich
half-time	Halbzeit(pause)

Another frustrating half hour passed without a single goal. But then, out of nowhere, the Liverpool captain made an incredible cross and the ball landed just metres from Chelsea's net, at the feet of Pete Alba. Alba kicked the ball and it flew towards the corner of the goal... Evie jumped out of her seat immediately. She knew that she had to try to see every detail if she was going to write about what had happened. But just as the ball flew into the net, a tall man in front of her also jumped up with his arms in the air and blocked her view while he celebrated the goal. Evie tried not to worry: she knew that they would show a replay of the goal on the large screens at every corner of the stadium. She watched the nearest screen very carefully.

cross	*hier:* Flanke
net	Netz, Tor
to block sb.'s view	jmd. die Sicht versperren
replay	Wiederholung
screen	*hier:* Videoleinwand
stadium	Stadion
to spin	sich drehen
abruptly	abrupt, ganz plötzlich

As Evie had expected, the replay was shown soon after the goal, and this time she made sure that she had a good view. She watched the captain's perfect cross again, watched Alba kick the ball, saw it spin in the air on its way towards the net... but then her eyes abruptly moved away from the ball. The ball was no longer important to her, and she did not care about the goal,

to come back into focus	wieder scharf werden
barrier	Absperrung
to separate	trennen
steward	Ordner

because she had seen something else on the screen. She was watching something near the net, but it wasn't the ball. It was a person.

"Connor." Evie spoke the name very quietly, as though it was not real. The world around her seemed to stop for a moment. Then she shouted out loud as everything came back into focus: "Connor! Connor!"

Carla looked at her as if she was mad. Evie only just managed to say a few words to tell Carla that she would meet her by the car after the match. Then she left her seat and ran towards the other side of the stadium. There were only five minutes left of the match: she simply could not lose Connor again as she had done at the concert.

This time, Evie had a good idea of where she could find Connor. In the replay of the goal on the screen, she had seen him in the crowd behind the net. She had noticed that he wore a red Liverpool shirt and that he had watched the ball go in before jumping up and down in celebration. She knew that she could get to him if she could just reach the right part of the stadium in time.

Evie moved through the crowd as quickly as she could. She reached a barrier that separated the part where she had been sitting from the part where she had seen Connor. She saw a steward come towards her. The steward called out for her to go back to her seat, but without even thinking Evie jumped over the barrier.

Now she was really close. She continued to move towards the goal until she could see Connor, not far away from her. He had not noticed her yet and was celebrating and singing with the other Liverpool fans.

final whistle	Abpfiff
to push past	sich vorbeidrängeln
dizzy	schwindlig
in desperation	verzweifelt

A moment later, they all began to celebrate even more as the sound of the final whistle rang in Evie's ears, meaning that Liverpool had won. But Evie did not feel at all like celebrating: the whistle also meant that the game was over. Soon everybody would leave the stadium. She felt sick and everything started to remind her of the concert where she had found, and lost, Connor before. The people who pushed past her brought back all the terrible memories of that night and Evie began to feel dizzy. She closed her eyes for a moment and told herself that Connor was not far away. This time, it had to be different!

Evie carried on pushing her way towards Connor's seat while the crowds moved towards the exits. Soon she reached the seat, but Connor had gone.

In desperation, she called out his name.

Just then, a boy in a red Liverpool shirt and cap looked at her. When his eyes met hers across the crowd, his face lit up in an enormous smile that showed the dimple on his left cheek.

ÜBUNG 26: Reading comprehension. Beantworte die Fragen zum Text!

1. Does Evie write down a lot during the match?

....

2. Why does it worry Evie that neither team has scored?

....

....

3. Who scores the goal?

....

4. Why does Evie not see the goal properly?

....

5. What happens when Evie watches the replay?

....

6. What does Evie do after she has seen Connor on screen?

....

....

It could not be anyone else but Connor – Evie did not only recognize his face, but also the wonderful feeling that instantly spread through her.
Connor jumped over the seats that separated them and gave her a huge hug. For a moment, neither of them could speak. Evie realized that words would be useless to describe how she felt, so she kissed him instead. He kissed her back and she shivered in his arms. They looked into each other's eyes as they finally pulled away from the kiss.
Connor paused for a minute before he managed to say: "I don't understand – you didn't call me after the holiday. I thought you weren't interested in seeing me again."
Evie felt very sorry. She explained how the rain had made his phone number impossible to read. She also explained about the night of the concert when she had seen him in the crowd.
"No way!" said Connor, smiling with surprise. "That's crazy! To think that we were so close but didn't meet. I tried so many ways to find you after you didn't call – if only I had known that you were so close to me that night."

ϟ No way!	Ausgeschlossen!
to save	*hier:* speichern

"Never mind," said Evie, "I've finally found you now, and I'm not letting you get away again! ...Which reminds me: can I have your phone number again, please?! And one other thing – what's your surname?"
"It's James," said Connor. "Connor James."

Before he had finished saying his name, he had already taken out his mobile phone, ready to save Evie's number. They both took each other's numbers very carefully and wrote them down as well as saving them on their mobiles. Connor even asked Evie to write down her number on his arm.

"Let's never lose each other again," he said softly and kissed her once more while the last of the football fans moved towards the exits.

Behind them, the same steward who had tried to stop Evie before smiled as he saw the happy scene.

But then Evie noticed that they were almost alone in the stadium. Even though Evie could not think of anything she wanted less than to stop kissing Connor, she remembered that Carla would be waiting for her. So she forced herself to pull away and told Connor that they should leave.

They walked out of the stadium together, holding hands, while Evie explained what she was doing at the match. In the middle of describing her work experience, Evie suddenly remembered something that made her feel very worried.

"Oh no!" she said and put her hand to her mouth. "I've just realized – I missed the goal completely! I'll never be able to write a good article about the match without describing the goal."

to calm	beruhigen

He saw how anxious she was and put his arm around her shoulder to calm her.

"Don't worry," he said. "I think I had the best view of that goal in the whole stadium. I can tell you all about it."

Connor described every detail of the goal, smiling as he remembered it. Evie quickly made a few notes to help her with the article. Then she spotted Carla in the distance, looking at her impatiently.

"Thank you," she said to Connor. "I have to go now, but you don't have to worry about me calling you this time! See you later, Connor James!"

Connor kissed her one last time.

"Bye, Evie Smith," he said softly.

ÜBUNG 27: Unscramble the text! Ordne die folgenden Sätze chronologisch.

a) Evie tells Connor that she saw him at the concert.

b) Evie and Connor tell each other their surnames.

c) Evie remembers that Carla is waiting for her.

d) Evie finds Connor's seat but he has gone.

e) Connor tells Evie that he will explain everything about the goal.

f) Evie and Connor look at each other without speaking.

g) Connor hears Evie calling his name.

1	2	3	4	5	6	7
d						

to contain	*hier:* zurückhalten
to spill out	heraussprudeln
↯ to dump sb.	mit jmd. Schluss machen

Evie ran towards Carla and the silence of her car, which seemed all the more strange and empty after the wonderful moments she had just spent with Connor. She felt that she could not contain her happiness any longer. A huge smile spread across her face.

"So, what are you so happy about?" asked Carla.

Evie had not meant to tell her about Connor, but the words just seemed to spill out of her. She told Carla all about how she had seen him on the screen and had gone to find him on the other side of the stadium.

To Evie's surprise, Carla smiled. Evie thought that Carla's smile looked strange, but then she realized that it was because she had never seen it before.

"That's a pretty amazing story!" Carla said. "A lot more interesting than the match!"

Evie laughed. She was shocked to realize that she was enjoying their conversation.

"Anyway, Evie," continued Carla. "I had meant to apologize for the way I've behaved towards you. I hope you know that it had nothing to do with you personally. To be honest..."

She stopped for a moment as though she did not want to finish the sentence. "...To be honest, I've been very upset because my boyfriend dumped me two weeks ago. We had been together for five years... it's been really hard."

Evie suddenly felt sorry for Carla. She had thought that Carla hated her when, in fact, she was simply having a difficult time herself.
Their conversation continued all the way back home. They talked about many things, but the one thing Evie found the most interesting was when Carla told her all about how she had become a journalist. By the time they arrived at Evie's house, Evie felt that she had learned a lot. She said goodbye to Carla and thanked her for taking her to the match. Then she ran into the house to find Olly.
"GUESS WHAT!" she exclaimed.

ÜBUNG 28: Missing words. Vervollständige das Gespräch zwischen Olly und Evie!

Evie: (1.) *G*.................. what!

Olly: I don't (2.) *k*................., what's happened?

Evie: I found Connor at the football (3.) *m*..................!

Olly: I can't (4.) *b*.................. it! How did you (5.) *f*.................. him?

Evie: I saw him on the (6.) *s*.................. .

Olly: That's incredible! Then what (7.) *h*.............?

Evie: I went to (8.) *l*.................. for him. He saw me when I called his (9.) *n*...............

Later, Evie called each of her three best friends to tell them what had happened. Of course, they wanted to know absolutely everything about it, so Evie invited them all to her house. Once everyone had arrived, they all started asking Evie hundreds of questions.

"Was he like you remembered him?" Holly asked, but Evie had barely begun to answer before Emily added, "Was he upset that you hadn't called?"

Eventually, Evie had told them every detail of her adventure, and they had asked every question that they could think of. Then suddenly, Evie remembered that Emily had also found romance through her work experience.

to ask sb. out	jmd. einladen
proudly	stolz

"How are things with Josh?" she asked her.

"Great!" Emily replied. "Really great. We still have so much fun at work, and now we've started to see each other after work, too. He's asked me out on a date this weekend in fact. You know, I think it must have been fate that my first placement fell through... things have really worked out perfectly."

This time, Evie did not argue with Emily's ideas about fate. After what had happened to her that day, she was not so sure of her opinion on that subject any more.

Evie spent all of Thursday morning writing her article about the match. She wrote slowly and carefully, and then proudly handed her article to Ian. He came back to her desk five minutes later and put it back in front of her.

ÜBUNG 29: Questions and answers. Welche Antwort passt zu welcher Frage?

1. ❑ Was he like you remembered him?
2. ❑ Was he upset that you hadn't called?
3. ❑ How did you find him?
4. ❑ Was he happy to see you?
5. ❑ Did you get his number this time?
6. ❑ When will you see each other again?

a) Of course! And now I know his surname, too!

b) I saw him on one of the big screens when they were showing a replay of the goal.

c) Soon, I hope!

d) Yes, he was exactly the same.

e) Yes, he was smiling a lot and he even jumped over some seats to get to me!

f) No, because I explained what happened.

"This is very impressive, Evie," Ian said. "You've noticed some things that even Carla didn't see."
Evie thought that that was not as surprising as it sounded, because Connor's view of the goal had been much better than Carla's.
"Not only are your facts excellent, but your writing style is really very good, too," Ian continued. "I'm going to ask you and Carla to work together to write the article that will be printed in tomorrow's newspaper."

Evie felt as if she was on cloud nine. She had found the boy of her dreams again, made friends with an enemy, and now her writing would appear in the newspaper after all. Things could not get any better.

impressive	beeindruckend
enemy	Feind
reunion	Wiedersehen
to brim over with happiness	vor Freude sprühen
to inspire sb.	jmd. inspirieren
to part	sich teilen, sich trennen
hazy	diesig, dunstig

She and Carla worked hard on the article that afternoon, but they also had fun. Carla bought some food for them both and joked with Evie about the real drama of the match, Evie's reunion with Connor. Furthermore, Carla told her that if she ever wanted to return to work for The Post when she was older, all she had to do was to call Carla and she would arrange it. At the end of the day, their article was finally ready to be printed and Evie was brimming over with happiness when she left the office.

She took her mobile phone out of her pocket and dialled a number which, for a long time, she had worried she would never get the chance to call.

Connor answered the phone. "Hi, gorgeous," he said.

She told him about her article and how helpful his description of the goal had been to her. She told him about Carla and how she had inspired her with the story of how she became a journalist. But most of all, Evie talked about how happy she felt.

"I know what you mean," Connor said. "I can't stop smiling at the moment! Anyway, I was wondering whether you were busy this weekend. I'd like to see you again soon, Evie Smith..."

Evie carried on talking to Connor while she walked away from the office. The clouds had parted and the late afternoon sun was shining, covering everything in a hazy orange light. The puddles in the street had disappeared, and the sun's warmth on Evie's skin reminded her of summer.

"I'd love to, Connor," she replied happily.

ÜBUNG 30: Seasons. Welches Wetter passt am besten zu deinem Charakter?

1. What would your perfect day be like?
   a) ❑ I would spend it enjoying the beauty of nature.
   b) ❑ I would relax on the beach in the sun.
   c) ❑ I would get warm by the fire and watch the snow falling outside.

2. What are your favourite types of food or drink?
   a) ❑ Eggs, vegetables and fish.
   b) ❑ Ice cream, lemonade and fresh fruit.
   c) ❑ Roasted meats and hot drinks.

3. What type of clothes do you like to wear?
   a) ❑ I don't have a favourite style – I like to wear any style or type of clothes.
   b) ❑ Shorts and T-shirts in bright colours.
   c) ❑ I love to wear warm jumpers, woollen hats and gloves.

4. What is your favourite colour?
   a) ❑ Green.
   b) ❑ Yellow.
   c) ❑ Blue.

Lösungen und Glossar

Lösungen

ÜBUNG 1:

1. skiing – snow 2. sunbathing – beach 3. camping – tent 4. bad weather – rain 5. swimming – sea 6. summer – sunshine 7. raindrop – race

ÜBUNG 2:

1. a 2. a 3. b 4. b 5. a 6. b

ÜBUNG 3:

Mostly a): You should think twice before getting a pet. You probably shouldn't try to look after anything bigger than a goldfish!

Mostly b): You sound like a great pet-owner. You have a lot of love to give to a pet, so a dog would be the ideal animal for you. You would give it the attention and care that it needs.

Mostly c): Your perfect pet would be exotic, like a snake or a lizard. Looking after something so unusual would be hard work, but you would be just the right person to do it.

ÜBUNG 4:

1. to pound 2. to disguise 3. despair 4. wetsuit 5. collar 6. to break up 7. to widen 8. frantically 9. protective

ÜBUNG 5:

1. caravan 2. surfboard 3. weather 4. grandparents 5. saved, danger

ÜBUNG 6:

a. something b. had c. Evie's d. without e. wrote

ÜBUNG 7:

1	2	3	4	5	6	7	8
g	*b*	*e*	*h*	*c*	*a*	*d*	*f*

ÜBUNG 8:

1. d 2. c 3. b 4. e 5. a

ÜBUNG 9:

1. richtig 2. richtig 3. falsch 4. falsch 5. falsch
6. richtig 7. falsch

ÜBUNG 10:

Mostly a): You are intelligent and interested in the world around you, so you would probably make an excellent scientist or doctor. Your talents can make a difference to the lives of other people.

Mostly b): You were born to create beautiful things! You should be an artist, musician, or perhaps a writer. You would rather be true to yourself than be rich.

Mostly c): You are naturally good at languages and attracted to foreign cultures. Your ideal job would allow you to travel and speak to people in different languages. Your interest in culture and your sense of adventure might also mean that you could be a great journalist.

ÜBUNG 11:

1. is going to be 2. waited 3. saw, went 4. were, saw
5. wrote 6. had started, found

ÜBUNG 12:

1. friendship 2. cheerful 3. apple 4. said 5. lake

ÜBUNG 13:

1. anxiously 2. quickly 3. strict 4. fantastic, nice
5. cheerful, cheerfully 6. quickly, stylish

ÜBUNG 14:

1. wildly – calmly 2. enter – leave 3. huge – tiny
4. front – back 5. bright – dark 6. cheering – booing
7. noise – silence 8. split second – forever

ÜBUNG 15:

1. The girls go to the concert by train.
2. They are queuing and soon the queue gets longer and longer.
3. It is difficult because everybody is dancing and jumping and there is not much space to move.
4. Evie feels confused and lost because she cannot find Connor or her friends in the crowd.
5. It makes Evie feel worse because she realizes that it is time to go home and she has no hope of finding Connor.
6. Evie thinks that because she only saw the boy for a moment.

ÜBUNG 16:

A	G	C	O	F	R	E	E	Z	I	N	G
X	S	O	A	K	I	N	G	C	P	K	D
F	U	N	U	A	J	P	C	T	C	Z	J
E	Y	C	S	H	O	U	T	F	A	U	O
N	E	E	H	I	Z	D	K	X	T	P	U
C	R	R	U	M	U	D	D	Y	K	I	R
O	O	T	H	P	R	L	S	H	O	B	N
R	N	G	D	L	T	E	A	R	S	L	E
E	B	O	V	E	Q	U	B	A	K	U	Y
N	C	H	N	J	A	R	S	I	R	O	E
F	B	A	R	H	Z	E	T	N	A	L	P

Horizontal: freezing, soaking, shout, muddy, tears
Vertikal: encore, concert, puddle, rain, journey

ÜBUNG 17:

1. falsch 2. richtig 3. falsch 4. falsch 5. richtig

ÜBUNG 18:

1. I'm late because there was a lot of traffic.
2. I'm sorry, my dog ate my homework.
3. I thought you already knew.
4. I haven't done it because I've been ill.
5. I didn't know you fancied him when I kissed him.

ÜBUNG 19:

1. for 2. out of 3. on, in 4. At, with 5. to 6. up

ÜBUNG 20:

1. richtig 2. falsch 3. richtig 4. richtig 5. falsch 6. falsch 7. falsch 8. richtig

ÜBUNG 21:

1. office 2. book 3. comforting 4. surfboard 5. exclaim 6. fashion

ÜBUNG 22:

1. decide – choose 2. strange – odd 3. suddenly – unexpectedly 4. confused – puzzled 5. rage – anger 6. tired – exhausted 7. happiness – joy

ÜBUNG 23:

0-14 points: It seems that you do not know this boy well enough to tell whether he fancies you. Try to find ways to talk to him more and give him a chance to fall in love with you.

15-29 points: It is difficult to tell for sure whether he fancies you, but there are definitely some good signs. Maybe it's time to be brave and ask him out?

30-40 points: Wow, this guy is head over heels in love! It sounds like he really likes you a lot. If you fancy him, too, you are a lucky girl – he is probably desperate to go out with you!

ÜBUNG 24:

1. holiday 2. frown 3. flirt 4. Liverpool 5. office 6. journalist 7. trousers
Lösung: article

ÜBUNG 25:

1. wasn't 2. hadn't 3. didn't, should've 4. you'll, don't 5. mustn't 6. I'd

ÜBUNG 26:

1. No, she doesn't because the match is not very interesting.
2. Evie is worried because it would be very difficult to write a good article about a boring match.
3. Pete Alba scores the goal for Liverpool.
4. Evie does not see the goal, because a tall man in front of her blocks her view.
5. When she watches the replay, Evie sees Connor by the goal.
6. Evie tells Clara that she will meet her after the match and then runs to find Connor.

ÜBUNG 27:

1	2	3	4	5	6	7
d	*g*	*f*	*a*	*b*	*c*	*e*

ÜBUNG 28:

1. Guess 2. know 3. match 4. believe 5. find 6. screen 7. happened 8. look 9. name

ÜBUNG 29:

1. d 2. f 3. b 4. e 5. a 6. c

ÜBUNG 30:

Mostly a): You are most like springtime. You have a fresh, lively personality and love to be outdoors, so your favourite season is when nature is at its freshest.

Mostly b): Your naturally cheerful, sunny personality makes it obvious which season suits you best – summer, of course! Just don't forget to use your suntan lotion!

Mostly c): You love cold weather, but that does not mean that you have a cold personality! What you really love is to cuddle up next to a nice warm fire when everything outside is cold and snowy!

Glossar

abruptly	abrupt, ganz plötzlich
accidentally	versehentlich
to admit	zugeben
after all	*hier:* dennoch
all of a sudden	plötzlich, auf einmal
to analyze	analysieren, untersuchen
anger	Wut
anxiously	*hier:* ungeduldig
apart	getrennt
to ask sb. out	jmd. einladen (zu einem Date)
at such short notice	so kurzfristig
at that very moment	genau in diesem Moment
to attract a glare	einen wütenden Blick ernten
audience	Publikum
background noise	Hintergrundrauschen
to bang	schlagen, knallen
barely	kaum
barrier	Absperrung
to be amazed that...	erstaunt sein, dass ...
to be aware of sth.	etw. bemerken
to beep	piepen
to be in despair	verzweifelt sein
besides	außerdem
to be supposed to do sth.	eigentlich etw. tun sollen
to be swept away	fortgespült werden
to be tired of sth.	genug von etw. haben
to block sb.'s view	jmd. die Sicht versperren
blurred	verschwommen, undeutlich
blurry	verschwommen

to blush	erröten
to break up with sb.	mit jmd. Schluss machen
brightly	*hier:* fröhlich, gutgelaunt
to brim over with happiness	vor Freude sprühen
to bully	drangsalieren, mobben
to button up	zuknöpfen
to calm	beruhigen
to cancel	streichen, absagen
cape	Umhang
caravan site	Wohnwagenpark
career	Karriere, Laufbahn
to carry out a task	eine Aufgabe erledigen
to catch sb.'s eye	jmd. auffallen
chat	Plauderei, Unterhaltung
to cheat	mogeln, betrügen
cheek	Wange
to cheer	anfeuern, jubeln
to cheer sb. up	jmd. aufmuntern
cheerful	fröhlich, aufgekratzt
chest	Brust
to clap	(Beifall) klatschen
collar	*hier:* Halsband
to come back into focus	wieder scharf werden
to comfort sb.	jmd. trösten
comforting	tröstlich, beruhigend
comment	Bemerkung
commotion	Tumult, Gedränge
to complete	ausfüllen, beenden
concerned	besorgt
confidently	zuversichtlich
conscious	bewusst
constantly	ständig
to contain	*hier:* zurückhalten
to crack a code	einen Code knacken
to criticize	kritisieren
cross	*hier:* Flanke

crumpled	zerknittert
crush	Schwarm
curly	lockig
current	Strömung
customer	Kunde/Kundin
damp	feucht
to dare	wagen
to darken	verdüstern, verfinstern
deep in thought	in Gedanken versunken
defender	Verteidiger(in)
determined	entschlossen
dimple	Grübchen
dingy	schäbig, düster
disastrous	katastrophal
to disguise sth.	etw. verbergen
to distract	ablenken
dizzy	schwindlig
dog lead	Hundeleine
to drag	schleppen, schlurfen
to dread sth.	etw. fürchten
ϟ to dump sb.	mit jmd. Schluss machen
editor	Redakteur(in)
effort	Anstrengung
embarrassed	verlegen
encore	Zugabe
enemy	Feind(in)
energetic	schwungvoll, energisch
enjoyment	Vergnügen, Spaß
enthusiasm	Begeisterung
essay	Aufsatz
eventually	schließlich, letztendlich
exasperated	aufgebracht, verärgert
to exclaim	ausrufen
exhilaration	überschwängliche Freude
face up	mit dem Motiv nach oben
to fade	schwinden, verblassen

to fall (fell, fallen) through	ins Wasser fallen
far too quickly	viel zu schnell
fate	Schicksal
ϟ to feel in the way	sich fehl am Platz vorkommen
to feel left out	sich ausgeschlossen fühlen
figure	Gestalt
filing	Akten ablegen, Ablage
final whistle	Abpfiff
flashing	blinkend, aufleuchtend
folded	gefaltet
to force oneself	sich zwingen
framed by	umrahmt von
frantically	hektisch, angestrengt
to freeze (froze, frozen)	(er)frieren
frosty	frostig
gap year	freies Jahr nach dem Schulabschluss
to gasp	nach Luft ringen
gig	Popkonzert, Auftritt
to giggle	kichern
gorgeous	umwerfend, großartig
gradually	allmählich
greying hair	graumeliertes Haar
to groan	stöhnen
grumpy	brummig, mürrisch
ϟ Guess what!	Stellt euch vor!
half-heartedly	halbherzig
half-time	Halbzeit(pause)
ϟ to have a crush on sb.	in jmd. verknallt sein
hazy	diesig, dunstig
head over heels in love	Hals über Kopf verliebt
to hold (held, held) sb. tight	jmd. fest umarmen
ϟ hols (holidays)	Ferien
household chores	Hausarbeit
ϟ How about...?	Wie wär's mit ...?
ϟ How on earth...?	Wie in aller Welt ...?

hug	Umarmung
impressive	beeindruckend
incredibly	unglaublich
indecisive	unentschlossen
in desperation	verzweifelt
inside out	verkehrt herum
to insist	beharren, bestehen auf
to inspire sb.	jmd. inspirieren
instantly	augenblicklich, sofort
in time with the music	im Takt der Musik
into the distance	*hier:* davon, weg
It's no good.	Es bringt nichts.
jaw	Kiefer
jealous	eifersüchtig
to join in	mitmachen
knight in shining armour	Retter in der Not
laboratory	Labor
lap	Schoß
ϟ lie-in	Ausschlafen
to lift oneself up	aufstehen, sich aufrappeln
to light (lit, lit) up	aufleuchten, strahlen
ϟ loads of	jede Menge
to lose (lost, lost) oneself in	sich ablenken mit
to make (made, made) out	ausmachen, erspähen
mark	Fleck, Mal
mess	Durcheinander
to mess around	herumalbern
messy	durcheinander, unordentlich
to mirror	widerspiegeln
miserable	unglücklich
to miss out on sth.	etw. verpassen
to moan	jammern, klagen
much to her surprise	zu ihrer großen Überraschung
to mutter	murmeln
to narrow one's eyes	die Augen zusammenkneifen
neighbouring	benachbart

net	Netz, Tor
never mind	was soll's, egal
no matter how	egal wie
notebook	Notizblock
not only... but...	nicht nur …, sondern (auch) …
ϟ No way!	Ausgeschlossen!
nowhere to be seen	nirgends zu sehen
nursery rhyme	Kinderlied
on cloud nine	auf Wolke sieben
on time	pünktlich
opportunity	Chance, Gelegenheit
out of tune	schief, falsch (singen)
pang	Stich, Anfall
to part	sich teilen, sich trennen
to pass	*hier:* sich zuspielen
to persuade sb.	jmd. überzeugen
placement	(Praktikums-)Platz
plenty	jede Menge
pointedly	demonstrativ, bewusst
to pound	pochen, klopfen
to pour down	herabströmen
premier league	Erste Liga
to promise	versprechen
properly	richtig, genau
protective	beschützerisch, fürsorglich
proudly	stolz
to prove	beweisen
puddle	Pfütze
to pull up	*hier:* anhalten
puppy	Welpe
to push past	sich vorbeidrängeln
to put school before boys	die Schule wichtiger nehmen als Jungs
queen of diamonds	Karodame (Kartenspiel)
to queue (up)	sich anstellen, Schlange stehen

to quicken	schneller werden
ragged	zerfetzt, zerlumpt
rather than	anstatt
to realize	erkennen, begreifen
refreshing	erfrischend
relief	Erleichterung
replay	Wiederholung
research	Recherche
restless	unruhig
to rest on	liegen auf, ruhen auf
reunion	Wiedersehen
to revise	wiederholen, lernen
ridiculous	lächerlich
to roll one's eyes	die Augen verdrehen
to rouse sb. from	*hier:* jmd. reißen aus
to ruffle	zerzausen
to save	*hier:* speichern
sb.'s heart sinks	jmd. rutscht das Herz in die Hose
scientist	Wissenschaftler(in)
to score a goal	ein Tor schießen
to scramble	hasten, stürzen
to scream	schreien, kreischen
screen	Trennwand; Videoleinwand
sensible	vernünftig
to separate	trennen
shape	Gebilde, Form
shelf	Regal
to shelter from	Schutz suchen vor
She wished that the ground would swallow her up.	Sie wünschte, sie würde im Boden versinken.
to shiver	zittern
shred of hope	Fünkchen Hoffnung
shriek of excitement	aufgeregter Schrei
to shrug one's shoulders	die Schultern zucken
sickening	scheußlich, ekelhaft

to sigh	seufzen
ϟ sis (sister)	Schwesterherz
ϟ sleepyhead	Schlafmütze
to snap	jmd. anschnauzen
to soak	durchweichen
soaking wet	klatschnass
to soften	mildern, abschwächen
spike	*hier:* Stachel
to spill out	heraussprudeln
to spin (spun, spun)	sich drehen
spitefully	gehässig
to splash	spritzen
split second	Sekundenbruchteil
to spot	erblicken, entdecken
to spread (spread, spread)	sich ausbreiten
to squeeze	drücken
stadium	Stadion
staff discount	Mitarbeiterrabatt
stage	Bühne
to stare at	anstarren
statistics	Statistik(en)
steward	Ordner(in)
to sting (stung, stung) sb.	jmd. kränken
to stretch	(aus)strecken
to struggle	Mühe haben, kämpfen
stuck	festsitzend
to suit sb.	jmd. passen, gelegen kommen
support	Unterstützung
ϟ sure enough	tatsächlich, wirklich
suspiciously	verdächtig
swaying crowd	sich wiegende Menge
sympathetically	mitfühlend
sympathy	Mitgefühl
tan	Sonnenbräune
text message	SMS
the less... the better	je weniger …, desto besser

training	Ausbildung, Schulung
translator	Übersetzer(in)
trapped	gefangen
to trickle	tröpfeln, rinnen
to trudge	trotten, sich schleppen
to trust sb. to do sth.	jmd. zutrauen, etw. zu tun
unbrushed	ungebürstet
uncertainty	Unsicherheit
unlike...	anders als ...
unlikely	unwahrscheinlich
versus	gegen
volunteer	Freiwillige(r)
to wag one's tail	mit dem Schwanz wedeln
ϟ washout	Reinfall
to wave	winken
to weather the storm	eine Sache (gut) überstehen
weird	merkwürdig
wetsuit	Neoprenanzug
When it rains, it pours.	Ein Unglück kommt selten allein.
whereas	wohingegen, während
to whistle	pfeifen
ϟ wicked	abgefahren, super
to widen	breiter werden
to widen in shock	sich vor Schreck weiten
to wind around	laufen um, sich winden um
to wipe	wischen
with mixed feelings	mit gemischten Gefühlen
work experience	*hier:* Berufspraktikum
to work out	funktionieren
to yap	kläffen
to yawn	gähnen